Grownup War

by

John Daniel

Pennycome Quick Press

Acknowledgements

I should like to thank Alexis Lykiard and Maggie Fisher for their diligent proof-reading; Michael Carter for his help and encouragement ; Michael Frayn for taking the time to read and respond; Gail Irwin for her professional comments on the cover-design; Brian Hartel, Henry Goldberg, Hilary Cramp and Michael Irwin for supplying biographical data; Alan Dent and Ken Clay editors of Penniless Press where this memoir first appeared online; thanks to Michael Harvey for designing the logo and my wife Jane Spiro for her loving encouragement, critical acumen and technical dexterity in rescuing me from the elephant-pit of computer-incompetence.

Published by Pennycomequick Press
Weir View
Weirfields
Totnes
Devon
TQ9 5JS

ISBN - 978 0 9504253 1 3

Copyright © John T. Daniel

Front cover pastel by John Daniel.
Photograph on back cover by Jane Spiro.

Printed and Bound by Short Run Press Ltd, Exeter

*for Marcus, Philip, Ivan, Jessica
and their children.*

*"The camel-driver has his thoughts
and the camel, he has his."*

Arab proverb

Contents

1	On the Beach	1
2	The Promised Land	8
3	Up West	15
4	Gas	22
5	Common Ground	27
6	Battleships	31
7	Blackout	37
8	Necessary Fictions	42
9	Love and Lust	50
10	Our Finest Hour	57
11	Pyrrhic Victory	63
12	Uncle Joe and the Neighbours	68
13	Ancestral Voices	73
14	Good Friday	82
15	Sticks and Stones	87
16	The Fez and the Khukuri Knife	93
17	Yakusu	99
18	Teachers	104
19	In the Gutter	111
20	British Bulldog	117
21	Sins As Scarlet	124
22	Jane	129
23	Rabbits	135
24	Personal Remarks	140
25	Stanley Gibbons	145
26	Friend or Foe?	150
27	Spitfire	153
28	Mass Production	158
29	Cobber	165
30	Ice Cream	170
31	Miners Not Pirates	173
32	Losses	176
33	11 plus	180
34	The Interview	186
35	Circumcision of the Heart	190
36	Guilty Men	197
37	Wintry Journey	202

1 On the Beach

It was late August and I was building a sandcastle on the beach at Sandown in the Isle of Wight helped by a small blonde girl with a pageboy haircut wearing a pink swimsuit. Behind me, in a line of deckchairs with their trousers rolled up and knotted handkerchiefs on their sunburned heads, a number of men including my father were discussing the possibility of war. Usually I didn't listen to grown-ups, whose conversation was impossible to understand, but these were only a few feet away and their voices were loud and emphatic.

"It's all talk, newspaper talk."

"It's not us Hitler wants to fight, it's the Russians."

The sea splashed in, filling the moat with satisfying realism. Dad and I had spent much of the afternoon building the castle with a red metal spade purchased at the shop on the promenade, where he had also bought me four paper flags that decorated each of the plump towers: the red cross of St George, the blue flag for St Andrew, the red diagonal for Ireland and a scarlet dragon with its tongue branching out in flames for Wales.

"He wants to be friends with us."

"We have a lot in common."

"Say what you like, the Germans make wonderful binoculars."

"And cameras."

"Best in the world."

Mum waded into the surf holding her box Brownie in its scuffed leather case.

"Hold hands," she said to me but I didn't want to hold hands with the little girl, who obligingly took mine. Mum snapped us and later mounted it in her snapshot album with "Sandown, 1939" written underneath, the last photo before six years of filmless war.

"And cars. Mercedes-Benz and Opel."

"Best there are except for Rolls Royce."

We didn't have a car but one of Dad's friends had driven us to Portsmouth where we caught the ferry. It was the first time I had been in a car.

The little girl and I were decorating the castle with seashells and seaweed but I was becoming irritated with her because she was dumping armfuls of seaweed indiscriminately over the walls. I pushed her and she ran off then returned with her wooden spade.

"I don't like all those uniforms," Dad said. "All that marching and swastikas."

There was a general murmur of agreement that the marching and swastikas were unfortunate blots on an otherwise admirable civilisation.

"Hitler's done a lot of good. You've got to hand it to him. He solved the unemployment problem," another deckchair put in. "More than we could do."

There were more murmurs of agreement. The sea was flooding over the tops of the moat into the central courtyard. If there was one satisfaction greater than building a sandcastle it was watching it being swept away. The towers started to slip sideways. The little girl hit them with her wooden spade and I pushed her so she'd stop. The deckchairs retreated up the beach another few yards and re-arranged themselves in line.

"Roads too. Autobahns straight as a die. Not twisting and turning like ours."

"Best roads since the Romans."

"It's the Jews he doesn't like, not us."

No one said anything.

"My brother's been to Germany. He says there'll be war."

That was my father talking about Uncle Norman, his younger brother. Uncle Norman was the voice of authority in our family and if Uncle Norman said there was going to be war there was certainly going to be one. Uncle Norman had studied chemistry at the John Cass Institute and had a first class degree with letters after his name. He spoke French and German and had brought back a metal knife from his camping tour in the Black Forest with Zimmerman stamped on the handle which was in our kitchen drawer.

There was a murmur of foreboding.

"Let's hope not. The last one was bad enough."

"We don't want any more wars."

There was general assent as the sea swirled around their ankles and one of the towers slid into the foam, the four paper flags plunging into the waves. I scooped them up and put them in my metal bucket. The little girl in the pink swimsuit was picking up all the shells and putting them in her bucket, an appropriation I decided was unfair. I gave her another shove and she brandished her spade at me before running off. The political commentators folded up their deckchairs and stacked them against the wall as we climbed the steps to the promenade. The tar was so hot I could feel it burning through the soles of my sandals. The men said goodbye to one another and Mum, Dad and I walked back along the promenade to the boarding-house.

One of the balconied hotels facing the sea was on fire and there were red and gold fire-engines in the road with hoses trailing across the tarmac. I had never seen a real fire before and it was frightening. "Stand back!" the policemen ordered and I realised anyone inside would be burned to death. A column of black smoke was pouring through the roof into the blue sky and the long windows on the front were exploding with the sound of falling glass; the road was full of broken panes and water from the hydrants. A tall fireman in a brass helmet was standing at the top of the turntable ladder aiming a jet of water into the flames. It was exciting and I wanted to watch but Mum didn't want to stop so we walked on back to the boarding-house.

At tea in the dining-room a man dropped five cubes of sugar into his cup and winked at me. I tried to wink back but I had only just learned and couldn't manage it properly. I was only allowed two lumps of sugar; we didn't have cubes at home, only the boring, granulated kind. I was told off for stirring my blackberries-and-custard round and round until it looked like the purple and yellow patterns on the covers of exercise books. There were so many rules and regulations connected with eating that it was almost impossible to get through a meal without trouble. I was not allowed to spin my knife to see who it pointed at to be shot in the morning or to make twisted faces in the back of the dessert spoon like a fairground mirror or to put my elbows on the table. Everyone in the room talked in whispers as though they were in church.

Afterwards we went into the next room where there was a tall picture in a gold frame of a nude lady with long hair holding a jug of water on her shoulder. I pretended not to take any notice because nobody else did. Everyone was talking about the war.

"The Royal Family's German," my mother said to a woman in a green dress from the next table sitting on the sofa. "They changed their name to Windsor because it sounded more English."

"Let's hope they won't fight one another if they're relatives." said the woman,

I knew my mother was an expert on the aristocracy and the royal families of Europe. "Queen Victoria married a German, Albert, the Prince Consort," she informed the woman.

"That's right. They named the Albert Hall after him."

"And the Albert Memorial," Mum said, "Queen Victoria never got over his death. I used to walk round it on my day off when I worked in London. I knew every blessed camel on it."

"Hitler's not royal," said the woman. "It might be better if he was."

"Then there's the Prince of Wales," Mum said. "He was friends with Hitler. He went to see him with that woman."

I knew who that woman was. It was Mrs Simpson, beside whose potential for destruction Hitler's almost faded into insignificance.

I sneaked another look at the nude lady with the jug.

"And the old Queen, Queen Mary of Teck. She's really German."

"Well," the woman in green said, getting up from the sofa, "I lost my fiancée on the Somme last time. And I wasn't the only one. It wiped out a whole generation."

We travelled back to Portsmouth on the paddle-steamer. I held Dad's hand and we climbed down the steep stairs to the engine-room to look at the pistons driving the paddles because my father always wanted to look at engines. We stood together on the perforated metal gangway and watched the steel pistons leaping backwards and forwards like fairground horses. There was a strong smell of oil and the long shining steel rods shone in the sunlight. Through the spokes of the paddles I could see bright blue sky with the gulls wheeling around. It was exciting watching the water boil up underneath us but I knew I'd be

drowned and disappear into the green whirling pool and waves of foam if I fell. I gripped Dad's hand tight. The steel rods under our feet bucked and reared driving the paddles and the foam boiled furiously; the smell of oil made me feel sick so I was glad to climb up to the fresh sea air on the top deck, where Mum was knitting.

My skin started to peel like a snake's with the sunburn and I pulled it off in strips, trying to see how long I could make each strip. "Don't do that!" Mum said and dabbed white camomile lotion out of a bottle on me. But I couldn't stop pulling it.

When we reached Portsmouth harbour there was a newspaper boy waving a paper in the air shouting. *"PM to address the nation tomorrow! Chamberlain to address the nation!"*

The next morning was Sunday and I was outside on the path with my red tricycle when I was told to come inside. We sat in a row on the couch in the dining-room with Bob lying on the carpet in front of us, his brown and white woolly ears spread out on either side. I loved Bob and told him all my secrets. Dad had his wellingtons on; he'd been digging the rockery in the back garden; Mum was wearing an apron because she was cooking the Sunday joint and there was a smell of fat that I didn't like coming from the kitchen. The yellow arc on the radio with its names of strange places on the dial was lit up in the corner of the room where it stood on a small table above a photo of Uncle Norman in his black gown. Chamberlain was explaining that the British ambassador in Berlin had handed the German government a note which said that unless we heard by eleven o'clock that Germany had withdrawn their troops from Poland there would be war.

I looked at the electric clock with the difficult Roman numerals on the mantelpiece. I could almost tell the time. It was past eleven.

"I have to tell you," Mr Chamberlain's squeaky voice said, "that no such undertaking has been received and consequently this country is at war with Germany."

Through the open front door I could see my trike on its side where I had left it on the path in the sunlight. There were some words like ultimatum I didn't understand but I knew something momentous was happening. I had seen a photograph of Chamberlain in *The Daily Express* holding up a note in front of a metal aeroplane.

"Poor man," my mother said, "he does his best. I wouldn't want his job."

This was what she always said about politicians and sometimes I wondered whether she'd been offered their jobs. Dad walked across and switched off the wireless as if he were switching off something important. "We shall see," he said grimly.

Later that morning an air-raid warden cycled past blowing a

whistle, then the sirens sounded, up and down like a snake for the Alert, a clear steady peal for the All Clear. But they were just practising. The war didn't start that day or even that week although I thought it might. Nothing else happened.

It never did on a Sunday.

2 The Promised Land

I was aware growing up that my father was more modern than I was. I enjoyed prowling around country churchyards reading inscriptions on the decaying tombstones. For him few pleasures were more satisfying than the Crittall's metal window-frames in the Capthorne Avenue house which he and my mother had purchased in 1933 for £615. "Look at that!" he'd exclaim, opening the bay window and swinging it back and forth. "Look how it swings open!" It looked like an ordinary window to me, but I had never dealt with sash windows and was not to encounter them for many years. In Bow sash windows were universal. The family house in Athelstane Road had sash windows that, according to my father, stuck in their grooves, broke their sash cords, squashed his fingers and threatened to guillotine him every time he leaned out to tell the cat's meat-man to leave the meat under the knocker. Crittall's metal window-frames put Rayners Lane at the cutting edge of modern technology. Sash windows were part of a left-behind Victorian culture which included jellied-eel stalls, public-baths and music halls. It was an environment that my father viewed with some affection but which he had no desire to return to. He regarded the East End as somewhere he had escaped from, a claustrophobic existence where it was necessary to have lodgers in order to survive. One possessed a wooden leg and stumped across the floor above their heads keeping them awake at night. The rooms were over-stuffed, over-ornamented and over-furnished. The velvet cover along the mantelpiece had silver balls dangling off it, a feature my father particularly disliked. Above all the East End was poor.

Malmesbury Road School which my father reluctantly attended until his fourteenth birthday, considered itself superior to the Roman Road School because its pupils wore shoes. Symbolically he constructed, at the age of seventeen, a thirty foot aerial - the highest radio mast in Bow at the time - to receive the voices of the outer world. The programmes from 2LO, the pre-BBC transmitter, crackled into Athelstane Road bringing the voices and music of the modern world.

After their mother died, the three children, Len, Norman and Dorothy – Doll as she was always called – ran the house letting the upstairs to lodgers who even when they had two legs were generally unsatisfactory. One of them stole a sirloin of beef from the kitchen cupboard and was chased down the street by Norman who engaged him in a stand-up fight to recover the Sunday joint. Norman took charge of the domestic accounts, called himself the Chancellor of the Exchequer and instituted a box with labelled slits in the lid for the utility bills and food. There were tempestuous arguments and cross-examinations between him and Doll on the price of sausages or a pair of kippers. My father, the eldest at 24 and the calmest in temperament, tried to adjudicate and gained a reputation as the peacekeeper.

He had already met my mother at a St Patrick's Day dance and bought her a gold shamrock brooch which she wore every St Patrick's Day for the rest of her life. They became engaged and began the laborious work of saving for their bottom drawer. My mother was taken to meet Lucy, the widowed mother whom she described as sitting in the window, a figure of grief unable to recover from the death of her husband George a year before. "She didn't want to live," was my mother's verdict. Lucy died a year later and was buried next to George in Bow cemetery. It seems to have been Norman who hit on the idea of my parents marrying as soon as possible and starting a home not only for themselves but for him and Doll as well. "You two get married and we'll come and live with you," he is reported as saying, "I need a better address." Rayners Lane was regarded as infinitely superior to the East End, and was advertised on the Underground as one of the leafiest countryside suburbs, practically a landed estate.

"What could I say?" my mother asked in later years when

people queried the notion that she should have started her married life with her brother and sister-in-law. "There was nothing I could do."

She was outnumbered; she had already stated her aversion to Athelstane Road, Bow and everything in it. Doll was only sixteen; there was no question of leaving her behind. There was that tight-knit family loyalty common to East-enders which my father shared. The family, whatever its ills or disputes, was indissoluble. The three siblings turned out to have very different politics and life-styles – even religious beliefs – but there was never any question of renouncing the family connection, strained at times though it was.

My father and his brother piled the horsehair chairs, the velvet mantelpiece-cover and other specimens of Victorian furniture into the small yard at the back of the Athelstane Road house and set fire to them. Only one piece of furniture passed the Rayners Lane test – the couch on which we were to sit in a row listening to Mr Chamberlain some six years later. The rest of the family heirlooms went up in smoke.

But modern living meant more than electric lights in every room and walnut-veneered furniture. It meant owning a home, a financial piece of wizardry that mystified my mother who couldn't understand how it was possible to spend £615 on a house when neither of them possessed such a sum. My father found out about mortgages and the builder's promise that £25 deposit down secured a home of one's own. Landlords, universal in Bow, disappeared with the Victorian furniture. "You pay rent all your life and have nothing to show at the end of it," was the collective wisdom on renting. Rayners Lane meant freedom from peg-leg lodgers and shuttling relatives who exchanged living spaces every year like musical chairs. Rayners Lane meant no more trips to the public baths with a bar of soap and a towel under your arm. The upstairs bathroom in Capthorne Avenue had hot and cold running water, black and white modernistic tiles and a lavatory with a chain.

To be sure Rayners Lane houses were not as modernist as the purists might have dreamed. There was the splendid new Underground station designed by R.H.Uren at the top of the small hill in the centre of the shops and there was the white modernistic Odeon with its curling top and powder-room that was the glory of the new shopping centre. A few streets away there was the brick and metal window-framed Roxbourne School that I was to attend. But the rest was all pseudo-Tudor with pebbledash, imitation timbers, bow windows and a spray of

stained glass in the front door. The thousand houses a year erected by a young builder in his twenties, Thomas Nash, on a tract of land purchased from Christ Church, Oxford for £60,000 and marked on 19th century maps only by marsh-signs was about as unmodernist as he could build them. The Devonshire street-names – Exeter and Lynton Road, Widdecombe and Lulworth Crescent, Torbay and Newquay were rurally romantic, although as my parents spent their honeymoon at Lynton in Devon they probably appreciated them. On the outside the houses had pitched roofs and beams like thousands of others but inside there were newly-plastered bare walls with smooth ceilings, decorated by a hanging marbled light-bowl supplied *gratis* by Mr Nash.

If the exterior didn't resemble one of the new ocean-liners, the interior might. My father set to work papering the walls with oatmeal paper and a thin dado strip of sober autumn leaves. Otherwise there were no ornaments on the mantelpiece, no statues or pictures, no photographs except Uncle Norman looking cadaverous in his gown under the wireless. Plainness was the watchword and although my father never actually banned porcelain shepherdesses and Alsatian-dog table-lamps it was understood that ornaments were part of the old, overstuffed Bow world that had been left behind. He fitted a stainless steel letterbox on the front door and installed a bell, that harbinger of modernism, to replace the brass knocker that the cat's meat had been left under. Everything was new: the shops, the streets, the red letter-box at the corner of Capthorne Avenue, the 114 bus, the streetlights, the sycamore trees planted at fixed intervals, the newly-weds, the families.

The families were as slimmed-down and modernist as the window-frames. Gone were the sprawling broods that filled the back streets of Bethnal Green and the Commercial Road. We came mostly in ones, occasionally in twos, rarely in threes. I was one, born in the front upstairs bedroom and according to later reports followed by my mother's pronouncement, "I'm never going through that again". Whether this was because I was male, a gender that my mother always had reservations about, or whether it was because my mother had little desire for motherhood and felt that one child was the minimum she could get away with is uncertain. Four years later the onset of war supplied a rational reason for not having another and postponed the decision for the duration and in effect for ever. My father in his democratic fashion stated that it was up to Mum. But Mum had had enough. One was more than enough, since I didn't require dresses or embroidered frocks which would go some way towards justifying my existence. "It's all men," she frequently said, referring to the world at large or to the fact that Norman had moved in and the two Daniel brothers naturally formed a bond. Or perhaps because her sister Marjorie had also given birth to a boy, my cousin Michael. Motherhood was not my mother's dream of identity. Doll was a teenager but my mother never had any intention of extending her mothering further than was absolutely necessary. When I was born two years later Doll was required to move out of the house to make space for the new baby. She gave up her tailoring apprenticeship which she had begun after leaving school and decided to train as a nurse, a decision that was certainly influenced by her need to find a roof over her head, since trainee nurses invariably lived in the hospital.

I was an only child, that problematic being who inhabits the grown-up world without being part of it, who misses the rough-and-tumble sharing of siblings and who is both in the limelight and out of it, the focus of parental attention and yet unable to share opinions with anyone else on the subject. I have always felt that brothers and sisters are essential for a full, human existence and there is something lacking in those who don't possess them. Solitude becomes a natural state and although those with siblings assure me that not all problems are solved by their presence, I can't help feeling that some deep connection with the rest of humanity can be made through brothers and sisters which friends and acquaintances can never supply.

In her desire to restrict her family to one my mother was of her time but otherwise her aesthetic tastes were not as uncompromising as my father's. One afternoon she brought back a framed print of a vase containing a bunch of red and yellow dahlias. "It's a splash of colour," she exclaimed to my father in self-justification, "I think it would look nice on the wall." It was a revolutionary statement given the bareness of the walls, but my father was never a tyrannical man. It was her home as well as his. The picture was hung on its small chain over the light oak dining table. Perhaps my mother appreciated his forbearance because she never bought another and the pot of red and yellow dahlias remained the sole representation of western art in our house.

But the breach had been made and in later years Uncle Norman sent back two brass storks with inlaid enamelled wings from India and Auntie Doll six ebony men paddling a dugout canoe from the Congo. Over the years the bare rooms gradually succumbed to the clutter of school-photographs, music-box chalets and cork-pictures that made the place look, as they say, like home. But my father never needed ornaments to express his feeling of home. Plain walls and Crittall's metal window-frames that swung open to the touch were his idea of utopia. He'd grown up in a Petticoat Lane of artefacts. Rayners Lane was his dream of Eden where everything was new and there were no neighbours knocking on the back door for half a cup of sugar. He had never heard of the Austrian architect Alfred Loos but he would have agreed with his pronouncement that decoration is a crime.

The onset of war and the Luftwaffe effectively stopped the spread of suburbs like Rayners Lane encircling London from Watford to the north, Brighton to the south Reading to the west and Southend to the east. After the war the Green Belt of the Underground posters and Metroland become a reality, at least for a few more miles and a few more years. Many heaved a sigh of relief and thanked God that Nazi bombs called a halt to the unstoppable march of the speculative builders. John Betjeman famously implored friendly bombs to fall on Slough and he might have added Rayners Lane. But John Betjeman was no modernist and had never lived in Bow.

There was a political dimension to my father's modernism. He always voted Labour unlike his brother and his wife, believing that social life would get better and better given free education, clean air and the widespread use of steel window frames. It was a belief he never abandoned. Rayners Lane was the first step to the Promised Land, and he had taken it.

3 Up West

My mother took me on a secret trip to London – Up West as she called it – and we walked through Hyde Park where there were anti-aircraft guns sticking out of the newly dug earth surrounded by sandbags and the hawsers of barrage balloons anchored in concrete blocks. Long cables were attached to the silver balloons that floated in the sky with floppy fins like elephants' ears. They were supposed to stop the Germans bombing us, but I couldn't understand why the German pilots didn't just fly around them. It was years before I discovered it was the wire hawsers that were the deterrent not the balloon, which was only there to hold the wires up.

I was not sure why we had come up to London, particularly as I was instructed not to tell Dad about our visit but it was an exciting place with statues of soldiers on horses with plumes in their hats. "London always gives me a lift," Mum said. "It does me good." We walked through the park to where there were cream-coloured houses four storeys high with long windows and black railings that had not been taken away as they had in Rayners Lane. We climbed up a flight of steps and my mother rang the brass doorbell. The door was answered by a maid in a white cap who led us into a large room with a high ceiling and tall windows. I was instructed to wait there and not touch anything. There were tall vases and shelves of leather books and long, dark-blue velvet curtains, bunches of flowers and a large mirror in an ornate gold frame. I stood in the middle of the thick carpet looking around until my mother reappeared holding a brown paper parcel and the maid opened the door for us. We walked back down the steps across the park to the Underground and then home, which we reached just before Dad came in from work. "What have you been up to?" he asked me as he always did. I wanted to tell him about the barrage balloons but I kept Mum's secret although I didn't like doing so. She told Dad we had been shopping but didn't say where. It was the first time I realised grown-ups didn't always tell each other the truth.

Mum often talked to me about her life as a lady's-maid before she was married. "It was the happiest time of my life, "she said, "I didn't have a care in the world." She told me her ladies took her to Scotland when the families went grouse-shooting and the South of France where she stayed in the Carlton Hotel in Cannes and saw the Battle of the Flowers in Nice. She had lived in four-storey Georgian houses in London in Hans Crescent and Sloane Street and Eaton Square.

"It was all wonderful," she said, "Rayners Lane was a comedown but I wanted to marry and have my own home and you can't do that and stay in service." The Rayners Lane neighbours were ignorant of the things my mother valued. They didn't know about the Season with the Eton and Harrow match or Ascot when there were parties with champagne and oysters or the Glorious Twelfth or Queen Charlotte's Ball when the debutantes were presented at Court, or Cowes Week when they raced yachts at the Isle of Wight. They only knew about the Oxford and Cambridge Boat Race which ranked fairly low on my mother's list.

She loved to talk to me about her years in service. Her first job was as a children's maid with Lord Rayleigh, a scientist who had discovered argon in the atmosphere. "All one wing was laboratories," she said, "and the drive was a mile and half long so there was nowhere to go on your day off." Lord Rayleigh employed a staff of fifty on his Essex estate and engaged my mother as a children's maid at £16 a year, a meagre salary even for the 1920's. "Bloodsuckers" was Dad's opinion of Mum's employers but Mum won't hear a word against Lord and Lady Rayleigh though she agreed that £16 as a yearly salary was not as generous as it could have been. "I wanted for nothing," she declared in their defence. "I had free board and lodging and the lady's clothes when she'd got tired of them." She even claimed she saved on her annual salary. "But you had to do as you were told," she would say, with the implication that my father with his Labour opinions would not have survived.

All my father's political arguments were outweighed by my mother's love of the glamorous life in Kensington and Chelsea. Dad only knew about the East End. My mother had taken him on a tour of the Dorchester Hotel in Park Lane when it first opened. "Do people live here?" he had asked, not being sure what such an enormous building was for. Hotels, especially those like the Dorchester, remained outside our orbit and as a child I can never remember staying in one.

My mother had escaped from what she regarded as the dreariness of country life as my father had escaped from the East End. "Bread on bread" was her neat summary of existence in her Essex village. "We walked backwards and forwards to church twice on Sundays. That's all we did." Her dislike of the countryside and English rural life was long-lasting. "Once I'd been to London I never wanted to go back," she told me on numerous occasions although later she admitted, "It's all right if you have a car," a mode of life that went with hotels and was as far removed. As she moved up the domestic hierarchy of servants from children's maid to lady's-maid she received the status accorded her position. A lady's maid was, next to the butler, the most important person in the household and entitled to servants of her own. "All waiting on one another" was Dad's caustic verdict when my mother explained that she had all her meals cooked for her and one of the housemaids made her bed each morning. "I couldn't boil an egg when I got married," she boasted to me proudly.

I was told vivid stories about the life below stairs which set out to imitate the festivities in the drawing-rooms above with a succession of balls and parties. There were the footmen, the first always called James, the second Charles, whatever their real names were. There were Christmas and New Year parties when the valet dressed up as a ghost in the cellars and terrified the parlour-maids. There was a scandal when one of the footmen taught a parrot to welcome her ladyship in the drawing-room with an hilariously obscene greeting. There were numerous invitations from chauffeurs to drives in the Rolls Royce around the country lanes which my mother accepted, dressed in elegant white coat and cloche hat.

"They thought they were the lords and ladies," my father observed, but Mum passionately defended her years in service. "I don't envy them their wealth," she would always reply, "they

give lots of people work," an argument that my father had to admit might be true. But my mother's allegiance went deeper than having a job. She followed the activities of the gentry in "The Graphic" re-living the debutantes' presentation at Court for which she dressed her ladies in three-feathered Prince of Wales headdresses and made their silk underclothes by hand, copying Parisian fashions from photographs in "Vogue". "You don't seem very interested in looking after children," Lady Rayleigh observed to her one day with some perspicacity. "You seem more interested in dressmaking." So my mother was enrolled in the Regent Street Polytechnic on her afternoon off each week to learn cutting-out and sewing at Lady Rayleigh's expense. She had discovered her natural talent and when she left Lord and Lady Rayleigh she remained in London at the vastly increased annual wage of £50 a year.

But the households were never as numerous again and the great establishments began to disappear. The First World War killed off most of the large households as it did their subalterns. Fifty servants proved to be exceptional, a vestige of Victorian and Edwardian splendour which to my mother's lasting regret was never to be seen again. Apart from the royal household, numbers of servants dwindled into the tens then to single numbers. My mother's wages went up but her career as a lady's maid followed a downward spiral into four and three-servant establishments. She lived in Cadogan Square and Hans Crescent and finally in the Hyde Park hotel, alone with her employers. The great houses were sold off or taken over by the National Trust and opened to the public. My mother considered such democratic evolution regrettable but consoled herself with the thought that the rightful owners maintained luxurious flats in Knightsbridge and Sloane Square. "They don't want the expense," she would explain to my father, impervious as always to his feelings on the subject of aristocracy about which she considered he knew little or nothing.

Her loyalty remained unswerving and in the 1926 General Strike she was commandeered to make tea for those aristocrats who volunteered to drive trains and buses while the unions were on strike. My father's opinion that she helped the strike-breakers and betrayed those workers whose wages had been reduced was met by her usual retort: "What else could I do?" she would say, "I had to do as I was told or I got the sack."

One of her employers was Lady Diana Manners, aged twenty-four, the same age as my mother. The two young women became as close as their social positions allowed and when Lady Diana's engagement was announced my mother was responsible for her elaborate trousseau - underclothes, going-away dresses, evening gowns. She was given an invitation to the wedding in St Peter's Church, Knightsbridge, a rare honour for a servant. And when a month later, the news reached her that Lady Diana had been killed on honeymoon in a car crash in India my mother shut herself in her room for three days and wept. "I thought I'd never get over it," she said, showing me the yellow newspaper cuttings and embossed invitation, and perhaps she never did.

Her knowledge of the landed aristocracy was extensive and her allegiance unswerving. She knew about the Princess Louise, Princess Victoria and Princess Maud and she passed on news of their engagements and marriages to my father and me who received the news in respectful silence. She was ecstatic about the beauty of Princess Marina who married the Duke of Kent and devastated by his death in a plane crash during the war. She felt compassion for King George currently reigning over us "because he never wanted to be king".

We listened to King George making his Christmas broadcast the first Christmas of the war, which we celebrated with Uncle Paul and Auntie Marjorie at their house in Beckenham. The king stumbled and stammered as he talked of the dark days ahead. I prayed that he would be able to start up again and negotiate the hurdles of consonants. It was an agonising performance. "Poor man," my mother says. "He never wanted to be king. If it hadn't been for that woman."

I knew it was Mrs Simpson again, appearing like Banquo's ghost at our Christmas feast. I felt that Mrs Simpson was responsible for the king's speech impediment.

Uncle Paul was a socialist. He didn't approve of the Royal Family. "They wouldn't wait in the rain to see you, Vi," he said to my mother. " Why should you wait in the rain for them?"

Everyone laughed.

"You and your old Labour," my mother replied. "There'll always be rich and poor, whatever you say."

At last the King reached the end of his speech with his "God bless you all". Uncle Paul continued to tease Mum. "Don't forget," he said, "only four inches in your bath, Vi."

Everyone laughed again but Mum didn't care. The king only had four inches of water in his bath because of the war and everyone was expected to have the same. The broadcast ended with the national anthem as if to celebrate the fact that the king had managed to get through his speech. When Grandad and Grandma were with us we all had to stand up and toast the King, including Uncle Paul, but as they weren't, we stayed seated. Some years we stood up and some years we sat down. "If he could have continued as Duke of York he'd have been happy," my mother said. "He likes being at home with his family doing jigsaw puzzles."

"*I'd* like to stay at home with my family doing jigsaw puzzles," Uncle Paul snorted, "but some of us have to fight in this bloody war." He was angry at being called up into the Tank Corps especially as Dad was in a reserved occupation because he was a toolmaker. "What do I know about tanks?" Paul asked everyone, "I'm a journalist."

Uncle Paul was sports editor of *The Daily Express* and earned a lot more money than Dad. On the wall was a drawing given to him by the cartoonist Giles showing a troop of soldiers sitting on the grass by a tank. One of the soldiers was holding up a loose tank-track saying, "He says there's a ticking somewhere". Giles had given it to Uncle Paul because he was waiting to be called up in the tank regiment.

My mother envied her sister because Marjorie didn't have to make her own dresses but could go out and buy them from Marshall and Snelgrove's or Swan and Edgar's. But she didn't envy the fact that her husband was being called up.

Shortly after our secret trip to London Dad found out about Mum's journey because she complained that the lady hadn't paid for the work she had done. This confirmed my father's belief that the aristocracy had always made its money on the principle that employees should work for nothing. "It's exploitation," he said. He sat down and wrote a postcard in bright red ink demanding prompt payment – "so all the servants can read it" he explained.

"I'll never get another order," my mother wailed but Dad sent it and the lady sent a cheque by return. Perhaps Mum was right too, because that was the last of our secret trips Up West.

4 Gas

Gas. The word had a terrible sound as if terror was built into it, like *Berlin* or *Germany*. It was a word which carried a legacy from the First World War, which was still vivid in the popular imagination. My grandfather, George Daniel, died before I was born but I felt I knew him because we possessed his mahogany writing-box with rolls of Italian lire and his medals on orange and blue silk ribbons. The writing-box contained his diary of the war, written in pencil in a red book that opened from bottom to top secured with a wide black elastic band of the sort I used to hold my socks up. One entry read:

"Piave 20/10/18 heaviest shelling either France or Italy lasting from 9 pm 20/10 to 4am 22/10

H.E
H.V
& Gas Shells
& Bombs."

We were to be gassed from the air as the soldiers in the last war were gassed in the trenches. Nobody would survive. The trench-war was out of date; the new war would be fought from the sky and civilians would be gassed in their millions. Every man, woman and child in the country would be issued with a gasmask. Strangely enough there was little panic at this prospect of mass-destruction although it seemed credible and possible. As with so much else, we accepted it with that equanimity and fatalism which greeted so many drastic changes in the opening stages of the war.

I was summoned to be fitted with a gas-mask in a church hall staffed by women of the Voluntary Service, wearing bottle-green uniforms and hats like Girl Guides. We were instructed to stand in a large circle and were each handed a mask in a cardboard box while two WVS women patrolled around the outside of the circle, pulling us about like rag dolls.

"How old are you?" one asked me.

"Six," I replied with my fingers crossed behind my back to protect myself against the sin of telling lies. The fires of hell were less fearful than having to wear a Mickey Mouse mask, which was the prescribed issue for under-fives. Apart from the grotesque ears and wobbly nose it stigmatised its wearer as an Infant, only one step up from a Baby. The WVS lady looked at me with suspicion but finally handed me a box with a grown-up mask inside.

"Put that on!" she ordered, tugging it out and holding up in front of me like a bedraggled octopus.

I pulled it on. The inside smelled rubbery; the heavy green metal end to the short trunk weighed it down so that I was unable to breathe. The transparent visor misted up. I couldn't see and was close to panic.

"You're to carry this at all times," the distant, muffled voice of the chief WVS officer commanded.

I felt I was drowning. I dragged the short snout skyward and succeeded in pulling the rubber above my upper lip and sucking in the cool, life-giving air. I was immediately seized by one of the green-hats. My head was jerked back by my hair and the mask replaced, the WVS lady running her finger round inside the rubber to make sure that I was perfectly sealed inside. She then yanked at the straps behind my head so that I was buckled into the mask and unable to escape. I gasped for breath while she placed her hand over the top of my head and produced an oblong piece of cardboard which she held against the base of the perforated metal trunk.

"I want you all to breathe in and hold the cardboard on the end of your gas-mask," the chief green-hat announced.

My cardboard fell straight to the floor. I felt as if I was about to expire. It was like being gassed.

"You tiresome boy!" my WVS advisor shouted giving my hair a violent tug. She stooped down, picked up the cardboard and rammed it against my short trunk. "Now breathe in properly!" I gasped for air since there was no alternative and the cardboard oblong clung to the end of the mask.

"Remove your masks like this!" another green-hat ordered and we were given a demonstration on the correct way to slide our thumbs under the straps and extract our chins. I was trembling and the inside of my mask was wet with sweat and smells of rubber.

"*When must you wear them?*" the chief WVS person demanded. We knew how to reply because grown-ups frequently asked questions to which they had just given us the answer. "*At all times,*" we chorused.

"Gas can kill you," the WVS lady goes on, "We are expecting it at any time and if you leave your gas-mask at home it will be your own fault if you are killed."

As everything was our own fault already, there was no reason to think that being gassed would be an exception. We re-packed our masks in their square cardboard boxes and marched out of the hall in the double-file we moved around in on these occasions. Once outside we broke into anarchic violence, the boys whirling the boxes around their heads and charging at one another like mediaeval knights. But the gas-attacks from the air forecast by the authorities never happened and no gas-canisters were ever dropped on England. After a few months we began to leave the cumbersome boxes at home. The girls' mothers stitched linen covers on their boxes and embroidered them with their initials and elaborate daisy-chains or strings of blue forget-me-nots. The boys kept the raw cardboard but they were not useful even as weapons. When I ran they bumped awkwardly against my knees, entangling my legs and bringing me crashing to the pavement. I dumped the box in the cupboard under the stairs with the piles of old newspapers and the shilling-in-the-slot meter.

The popular explanation was that the Germans were frightened to use gas because they knew we would retaliate in kind. "Jerry knows what will happen" everyone said. "They're scared to use it." There were memories of blister gas and mustard gas and chlorine but gradually people realised it was not to be one of the weapons of this war.

Gas was regarded as the unused weapon of the Second World War and the gas-masks issued to all British citizens were seen as totally separate from the gassing of six million Jews in the Nazi death-camps. But the decision to use gas was taken by men who fought in the First World War and were familiar with its effects in the trenches. Hitler himself was gassed by the British. Five weeks before the end of the war near Werwick, south of Ypres, the British released canisters of chlorine gas. Hitler lost consciousness and by the time he reached the hospital at Pasewalk near Stettin he was completely blind.

My childhood experience with gas was also traumatic albeit on a smaller scale. I developed a technique of clambering up the stairs rapidly on hands and knees, only to slip on one occasion so that the edge of the step crashed into my mouth and knocked out several front teeth. They dangled up and down like yo-yos on strings of blood. It was not a spectacle that my mother could easily cope with. For her the first-aid aspect of motherhood was the most appalling part of an unsatisfactory role. Mouthfuls of blood, a wailing child and bouncing teeth compelled her towards the front door and out into the street where she seized the first passer-by – an elderly woman on her way to the shops. My mother dragged her back into the kitchen where I was sitting on a chair, conscious that I was at the centre of an important drama. But the woman was capable and efficient, and with the help of scissors and a bowl of warm water, my injuries were soon staunched. The stumps of my teeth remained a problem however.

"He should see a dentist," the woman said.

I have never been to a dentist before and was unprepared for what happened. "I think we should use gas," the dentist, Mr Sutterby said, producing a black rubber plunger, not unlike the one used by my father to clear the kitchen sink when it was blocked with tea-leaves. Mr Sutterby approached me holding the plunger in one hand with the clear intention of clamping it over my nose and mouth. I moved the other way and was held as I rose upwards, flailing my arms in a desperate attempt to escape through the ceiling while Sutterby pursued us both around the room waving the black rubber plunger, attempting to cover my nose and mouth. Eventually he cornered me and I succumbed to what was a terrifying attack, slipping into a blackness which did not expunge the trauma of the experience. I made sure I never had gas again.

5 Common Ground

The shelters went up, overnight it seemed, along the street - raw-brick oblong blocks without windows but with flat, tarred roofs and a single entrance with a slatted wooden door that was always padlocked. My mother flatly refused to use them.

"I'm not going to sleep in those," she announced, "they're common."

"Everyone's supposed to sleep in them," Dad said. "That's what they're for."

"You can sleep in them if you like," Mum declared, "I'm staying in my own bed." My mother made her sleeping arrangements part of her personal vendetta against Hitler. Hitler was a common little man, no more than a corporal in the last war. "He's not going to make me get up in the middle of the night. I'm staying in my own bed."

I began to realise that common was a complex word with a multitude of meanings. The shelters were common not only because everyone could use them but because the inside was full of stagnant water and the outside walls were decorated with the figure of Chad, a bulbous-nosed character peering over a wall with *Wot No Butter?* or *Wot No Bombs?* painted underneath. It was common to write on walls or to say What and even more common to spell it that way. Common was something you had to protect yourself against because it was everywhere. Mrs Beeson, only three houses away, was common, although my mother said she had a heart of gold. Mrs Beeson worked in the off-licence, which was a bit common and wore trousers and a headscarf, which were also common and smoked as she ran along the street and shouted "Hullo Vi!" to my mother over the hedge, which was the most common thing of all.

My mother's dislike of the street shelters was shared by everyone else in Capthorne Avenue so that they remained virtually unused. There were private, uncommon shelters on offer for those who could afford them: the Anderson, named after John Anderson, a Cabinet minister and the Morrison, named after another Cabinet minister, Herbert Morrison. The Anderson was designed for the back-garden and had a two-step entry into a semi-circle of corrugated iron covered with soil. The Morrison was an indoor heavy steel structure with zoo-like square mesh down one side. Both had their uses for us. My cousin Michael possessed an Anderson in his back-garden which served as an authentic underground headquarters with rusty water dripping through the roof and John Brown had a Morrison in his dining-room, providing a vast flat surface which could be used as a race-track for metal cars or an aerodrome for Dinky planes. There were also shelters at Roxbourne School, long concrete tunnels under the dug-up playing fields into which we were herded when the Alert sounded. We sat facing one another across the slatted walkway with our hands on our knees singing a medley of songs orchestrated by Miss Jessy. The sound wavered up and down the long tunnel disappearing into the small circle of light at the end. "D'Ye Ken John Peel" and "The British Grenadiers" were my favourites with their rousing choruses, followed by "A Froggy would A-wooing go" and ""Bobby Shaftoe's Gone to Sea" with "While the Moon Her Watch was Keeping" as a plaintive, lyrical finale. I discovered I couldn't sing in tune – a lifelong trauma – but I enjoyed these sing-songs in the shelters more than any other lesson.

My mother fought her personal war by staying in her own bed while the house rocked with the noise of shelling and Dad, Bob and I crawled into the cupboard under the stairs. We dragged our blankets, sheets and pillows into the narrow space with the sloping roof and attempted to make our beds between the gas-meter and the empty beer-bottles while Bob shuffled around in a circle on the newspapers. "He's trampling down the grass to make a bed," my father explained, "that's what he would have done in the wild." Bob was not happy with the sudden shafts of bright light from the searchlights and the crash of exploding shells. He threw back his head and howled with a strange eerie sound I have never heard him make before. I held his head under my arm and stroked his forehead in an effort to calm him.

Rayners Lane was not a prime target for the German pilots although there were munitions factories a few miles away at Park Royal and Acton. There was more danger to us out on the streets from the shrapnel of exploding British shells. In the morning after a raid we patrolled the gutters collecting pieces of the grey, jagged metal which we valued as highly as marbles or cigarette-cards. After a night of raids my mother would come down the stairs announcing triumphantly, "I didn't lose a wink of sleep," with a touch of superiority over those of us who had crept under the stairs. Sometimes my father tried to describe the dangers of being bombed – incendiary sticks that fell on the roof spouting fire and going through the floors of the house like a knife through butter, or the power of a blast that blew out all the windows and carried the heavy Victorian sideboard in my grandparents' house in Ipswich the length of the garden. But my mother refused to give in to such scares. "It's best not to think about it," she maintained. Her attitude fitted in with the nation's stoicism. "Britain Can Take It" was the watchword exemplified by the Queen's comment that she was glad Buckingham Palace had been bombed because she could now look East Enders who had lost their homes in the face. Much later I heard of incidents such as that of a young woman hurled into the air by blast, coming down skewered on a broken-off lamp-post where she hung in the air like a piece of burning meat. But such incidents were never reported - hysteria did not officially exist and even if I was not terrified, I was happy to sleep under the stairs with Bob and Dad, although it meant dragging our blankets and pillows up the stairs again in the morning.

One afternoon John Brown discovered that the shelter in King's Road had been left open and invited a select audience of his friends to view his younger sister, Sally's genitalia at a cost of threepence entry-fee. Three of us paid and stood in the semi-darkness between the unpainted wooden bunks. It was a thrilling moment. Prompted by her brother, Sally lifted up her skirt, pulled down her dark-blue knickers then lifted up her skirt again so that we could all inspect. We peered through the gloom at the small triangle at the top of her legs. It was not sensational.

"There's nothing there," John Martin said eventually.

He was right. There seemed to be nothing there except Sally's five-year old legs. Although I'd not known exactly what to expect the result was certainly anti-climactic.

John Brown said nothing and Sally continued to stand there holding up her skirt with her knickers around her ankles. We leaned forward to examine the situation more closely but even in the gloom of the shelter it was obvious that a small white triangle of Sally's anatomy was all there was to view.

"It's a swiz," Brian said, directing his criticism at the showman rather than the show. "It's not worth it." We all agreed. We had been led to believe that our threepences would introduce us to something sexually sensational and this spectacle was less than satisfying. But John Brown was a natural showman and he stood there with the silence of an impresario who did not need to justify himself.

"I want my money back," Brian said.

It was a decisive moment. We all wanted our money back. Threepence was not a negligible sum to be wasted on such a non-event. John Brown, however, refused to give us the refund we demanded. He clearly felt he had justice as well as nature on his side. "It's not my fault," he said. Sally dropped her skirt and pulled up her knickers as the disappointed customers were ushered out.

The shelters remained remote and unused, too high to climb and their flat, tarred roofs held our balsa-wood gliders, parachutes, cricket balls and other treasures as securely as if they had been confiscated by teachers. Only in the last months of the war when the heavy iron demolition ball crashed down on the flat roofs reducing them to rubble did we glimpse our treasures from the past six years slide momentarily into view before plunging into the dust and bricks of the unloved shelters.

6 Battleships

Six months younger, my cousin Michael was my superior in everything that mattered, climbing trees to a height where they started to bend towards the ground, building intricate dams that created lakes, hammering the lids on treacle-tins filled with water and hurling them into the bonfire so they exploded with exhilarating force. Michael was resourceful and anarchic, my ally against the grown-up world and my most treasured visitor especially since his father has been called up into the Tanks regiment and posted to North Africa.

"I don't know how I'm going to manage," Marjorie complained to my mother. "If ever a child needed a father, it's Michael."

They were visiting us from Beckenham in Kent where we had spent the first Christmas of the war and where our alliance had been forged. On Christmas morning we had sat up in bed on either side of Uncle Paul who tilted a tray full of toy cows and sheep up and down on his knees, making mooing and baaing noises in his Devonshire accent with great gusto as they slid from one end to the other.

"There you go me lovers!"

He often called us me lovers or me darlings.

The war news was coming in all the time. The German battleship the Graf Spee had been cornered by H.M.S Exeter and other British battleships at the mouth of the River Plate in South America. After a few days of mounting excitement it was announced that the Graf Spee had been scuttled, a confusing word that I associated with the coal scuttle. The Graf Spee was a pocket battleship, another confusing word which the Germans used to evade the restrictions on battleship-building laid down at the Treaty of Versailles. It was the first great sea victory of the war and we all thought the war would soon be over. Michael and I woke up at four o'clock in the morning to empty our bulging pillowcases, much to Uncle Paul's annoyance who swore and shouted, "Bloody Christmas! Why does anyone have Christmas!"

Now he was in North Africa and sent us two metal cap-badges of flat, silver tanks with pins in the back that we pushed through holes in our caps. Michael came to stay in his pink preparatory-school cap and blazer, and discovered in the first few hours that it was possible to climb out of the bathroom window, along the drainpipe and into the back garden.

"What can I do with him?" Auntie Marjorie asked my mother. "He's like this all the time. I don't know which way to turn." Life became much more thrilling when Michael was around. A pale-faced, frail-looking boy he seemed practically indestructible. I was inclined to be cautious and fearful of physical injury. Michael invented a new game of jumping off the shed roof, a bone-jarring leap that took all my courage and one I would never have performed without his example.

The war was becoming more dramatic. Hess, Hitler's second-in-command, flew to Scotland to meet with the Duke of Hamilton and other aristocratic friends he had known before the war, allegedly to conclude a separate peace between Germany and Britain. But he lost control of his Messerschmitt, crash-landed and was arrested. The incident was treated as evidence of Hess's instability. "Hess is mad" was the verdict in our kitchen where my mother was discussing the news with Marjorie. Peace was now beyond the realms of possibility. Hess remained a silent, enigmatic figure from the day of his flight to the day of his death. Churchill's war-speeches were characterised by a powerful pro-war rhetoric and Hess served as a focus for the madness of stopping the conflict, a solitary figure in the years that followed who appeared in the Nurenberg trials after six years confinement when he was sentenced to life imprisonment in Spandau prison until, at the age of 93 he hanged himself, as he had attempted to do a number of times previously.

Michael and I were committed to hostilities in our own fashion. It took the form of building elaborate wooden battleships, specifically H.M.S Hood and the Bismarck which we constructed in the shed at the end of the garden. We slept in the same bed, head-to-toe, and rose at dawn to begin hammering nails into long lengths of wood that were the hulls of our battleships. Our naval construction consisted chiefly in banging several pounds of nails into each vessel then arming them with brass corner pieces, bolts, nuts and any other fixtures that my father kept in round tins on a shelf over the bench. By the time we had finished, the battleships exhibited a porcupine appearance bristling with masts, gun turrets and lifeboats. With reels of cotton we created ship's railings and wireless aerials; finally we painted each ship in a grey-and-black-camouflage that we were too impatient to let dry. The paint dribbled across the bench, our hands and our clothing.

"We should sail them," Michael proposed.

"Where?"

"In the bath."

We carried H.M.S Hood and the Bismarck into the house. Michael had brought a tin of blue paint from the shed with which he proceeded to paint the bottom of the bath to give it a fjord appearance, he explained. The paint floated to the surface in oily circles, mixing with the grey and black of the hulls as we launched them down the sloping back of the bath.

Unfortunately both the Hood and the Bismarck immediately turned upside down, made top-heavy by the heavy armament of their superstructures. "They need keels," Michael said decisively so we carried the boats back to the shed, hammered a few pieces of steel underneath the hulls and brought them back to the bath. This time they listed heavily to one side. It took a number of trips, trailing water and paint, before we achieved upright stability. "The Hood gets sunk," explained Michael. "It blows up and the Bismarck escapes." We enacted the salvos from the Bismarck and the sinking of The Hood with considerable effectiveness. "Then the Bismarck gets bombed by Swordfish from The Ark Royal and sinks," Michael informed me and we improvised a variety of bombs and depth-charges.

Our war-games were interrupted by Michael's mother who emerged from her bedroom and began shouting at she opened the bathroom door and discovered the mayhem of the battle-scene. "We'll clear it up. It's only paint," Michael protested but Marjorie was in no mood for negotiation and my cousin was dragged around by his hair and scrubbed at the kitchen sink.

It was perhaps his experience of violence with the scrubbing brush at the kitchen sink that a day later prompted him to hammer a nail through a caterpillar as it crawled across the wooden surface of the bench.

I shouted but it was too late. The body of the caterpillar twisted convulsively on the nail and a yellowish-green liquid spurted out. It was not a species of caterpillar that I was particularly attached to, preferring the bushy, white-haired ones that shuffled endearingly along. This was a black, stick-caterpillar with feet at either end of its arching body.

"Why did you do that?" I demanded.

"It was disturbing me," Michael grinned, giving the head of

the nail another thwack. "It won't now." The caterpillar went into its final spasms on the nail.

I was undoubtedly influenced by my father's instructions not to kill anything and in my righteous, non-violent anger I launched myself at Michael, twisting his head under my arm and trying to bang it against the sharp edge of the bench. Michael responded by kicking me as hard as he could on the ankles so that I was forced to continued my campaign against violence by wrestling him to the floor where we rolled back and forth until separated by his mother who dragged her son from the shed, locking the door and forbidding him to enter it again for the duration of his visit. We were instructed to sit down and read a book.

Reading books was not Michael's forte, but he disappeared into the house and eventually reappeared with the unlikely choice of *The Life of David Livingstone,* proposing that we sit on top of the shaky pergola trellis which had been constructed to carry the garden roses. We sat precariously on the topmost cross-trees among the thorns to read the story of the Scottish missionary and explorer that Michael passed me to read; it was the only skill in which I had some measure of superiority and although a low-level activity it did have its occasional uses. I began reading aloud, beginning with Livingstone's birth in a Scottish village and continuing until I reached the moment when he said goodbye to his family to sail for Africa. Michael's eyes were suddenly full of tears. "What's the matter?" I asked but he was too upset to explain. His father's departure had been triggered again by the story which was perhaps why he had chosen it.

We abandoned reading and several days later found our way back into the shed and unearthed a large can of geranium-red paint from under the bench. Michael levered the rusty lid off with a screwdriver and we probed the surface which was covered with a thick, rubbery skin that could be pierced with a screwdriver, cut round the edge and lifted out. It was glutinous scarlet paint of a vivid hue that had a hypnotic quality about it and we sat on either side of the can facing each other, plunging our hands in, squeezing the skin and daubing it over our arms and faces. By the time we had finished no amount of scrubbing with turpentine could remove the paint; the scarlet traces remained under my fingernails for months, and I felt a mysterious kinship with it, long after I walked with my parents up to the Underground station and said goodbye to Michael. I treasured it as a blood-bond with my cousin and was sad when finally it faded into ordinary, boring skin.

7 Blackout

We were ordered to black out. My mother made the blinds on her sewing-machine and my father constructed the wooden grooves in which they ran up and down. This parental cooperation was a triumph and produced a blackout definitely superior to the neighbours, whose slivers of light shining through their curtains and tacked-up blankets attracted the air-raid wardens like moths to the flame. We were in total darkness.

It was a Stygian world. The lights in the street lamps were switched off or painted black so only a yellow spot the size of a sixpence shone through. On the Underground platform lamps were dimmed and inside each carriage dark blue bulbs made the seated passengers look like a row of corpses. The few cars on the roads were restricted to slits of yellow in their headlights. My father cut out a circle of black paper and inserted it into his bicycle lamp as instructed by the Ministry. Torches and flashlights were similarly masked and the names of Underground stations reduced to minute letters, a tactic that irritated my mother who was unable to read them in the dimmed platform lamps.

"How am I supposed to know where I am?" she demanded.

"You're supposed to know where you are already," Dad explained. "It's so the German pilots won't be able to read them from the air."

"I never heard such nonsense. They know perfectly well where they are. They have their maps and instruments. They probably know every town in England."

Seeing in the dark was not one of my mother's natural abilities. On the walk from the Underground, she bumped into trees, stumbled off the curb and crashed into the pillar-box at the corner of Kings Road and Capthorne Avenue. "This dratted blackout!" she shouted. It was the nearest she ever came to swearing.

The lights may have gone out in 1914 as the Foreign Secretary is supposed to have said, but they had been relit in the 1920's with a brilliance my mother never forgot. She loved the lights of London and adored window-shopping in the illuminated displays of Harrods and the new wrap-around windows of Peter Jones in Sloane Square. She talked of the pre-war decorations in Oxford Street and Regent Street with plaintive nostalgia and would clap her hands with delight recalling them. London was a world of light that had been snuffed out with brutal abruptness. Whatever the historians may say about the poverty of the 1930's they were the diamond-glittering years for my mother, light-studded as a dance-sequence by Fred Astaire and Ginger Rogers, glitzy as the mirror-balls she danced under at the Lyceum in the sequin dresses she made and the shoes and headbands she wore. "I sewed every sequin on by hand myself," she told me. Now it was all gone. Not only the electric lights but the theatrical shows that were festivals of light – "Showboat", "The Student Prince" and "The Merry Widow" which my mother considered peaks of perfection never again to be equalled. They had all been plunged into blackness.

My father's attempts to be philosophical only made matters worse. His suggestion that we should walk along the cliff-top by moonlight when we were on holiday my mother considered absurd and dangerous. Dad would theorise about our ability to see at night as we were walking back from the Underground.

"When all this was swamp," he'd say, "and we were out hunting at night, we found our way by the stars. Look!" He pointed out the North Star and the Plough. "We'd know where to go without any lights at all."

My mother wasn't interested in the constellations.

"I'm not out hunting," she'd say, " I just want to get home."

Dad was always intrigued by our animal qualities and our connection with the animal world.

"We've lost our ability to see in the dark," he declared.

"Modern civilisation has blunted our faculties. We need to relax with the darkness, then we can see as clearly as other animals."

His speculations about our affinity with animal-life were of even less interest to my mother than the position of the stars.

"We're really animals with clothes on," he'd say. "Look at babies in their prams. You can see by the way they clench their hands above their heads they're trying to reach for the branches."

"I never heard such nonsense," Mum replied.

"It's the same with our ability to see at night. We've evolved from animals who found their way at night instinctively."

The word evolved suggested the works of Charles Darwin, a writer whose books my father had never actually read but in whose theories he devoutly believed. My mother took evolutionary theory as an affront and made indignant protest:

"*I'm* not an animal," she retorted. "You may be but I'm not."

"We all are," Dad insisted. "I can't understand how you can believe all those stories about Adam and Eve."

"Lots of very clever people do," Mum would reply. "You and your Darwin."

At such times I thought my mother associated Darwin with the blackout as surely as she associated God with Genesis and light. Sometimes I thought she blamed Darwin for the blackout and the war.

It was not just the blacked-out lamps that my mother disliked but the colours of war, the drabness of khaki uniforms and the dullness of ration-books. She hated the sandbags that were banked outside buildings and the camouflage scrim draped over pillboxes. For her the war was the absence of colour and light.

One evening when I was alone in the house I heard a warden shout, "Get that light out!" I rushed around the rooms checking the blinds were down, then ran upstairs and observed a sliver of light underneath the door of my parents' bedroom. But I hesitated before bursting in. The parental bedroom was not just another room into which I could charge whenever I felt like it. It was hallowed ground that I trod on only once a week on Sunday mornings when I carried my parents a morning cup of tea and the *Sunday Express*. The sanctity of Sunday and all it stood for hung over it as well as a mysterious, erotic air. Stockings were draped over the backs of chairs and there was a scattering of powder on the dressing-table and a seductive trace of perfume. A dressing-table with three full-length mirrors captured me from the sides in a disturbing fashion whenever I ventured near. The double bed and the wardrobe were of figured walnut veneer with a swirling grain that was more expensive than anything else in the house. It was not a place to be violated without penalty, but the situation was extreme. *"Get that light out!"* shouted the warden emphasising his words with a thundering kick against the front door. I abandoned my hesitation and rushed in, spotting immediately the offending light dangling above the bed. To reach it I would have to climb up onto the bed and march across the billowing eiderdown. *"Get that bloody light out!"* bellowed the warden's voice again accompanied by renewed kicking at the door. I launched myself, jumped on to the eiderdown, marched over the soft waves in time with the beating of my heart and clicked the switch off, relieved to hear the warden's retreating feet in the darkness.

Next morning my father discovered the line of dents caused by the warden's steel-capped boot in the painted surface of the door.

"How did these get here?" he asked me.

I decided it was simpler to deny all knowledge of the incident than go into involved explanations. "I don't know," I said.

"You must know. You were in the house last night. These are the warden's hoof-marks." I was intrigued that he called them hoof-marks as if the warden were a horse and peered at them thoughtfully. "You must have left the light on."

I decided that it was too late to attempt an explanation and said nothing.

"Why would he kick the door otherwise?"

I remained silent, aware that my non-explanation compounded my guilt. My father filled the toe-marks and repainted the surface, but I could still see the faint indentations under the surface, recalling the truth that had somehow twisted itself into its opposite.

The blackout seemed at one with the black-and-white images of the war years. The Gaumont newsreels at the cinema presented us with images of convoys steaming across a grey Atlantic to the final black-and-white stick figures bulldozed into black holes in the death-camps. The patriotic photographs that captured the spirit of resistance – the dome of St Paul's rising from a pall of black smoke, the milkman picking his way through the rubble delivering the morning milk were in shades of black and grey. The grainy texture matched the grimness of the period. When coloured film of Spitfires or of Hitler with his dogs at Berchtesgaden were shown after the war they seemed inauthentic. The most memorable images were of a Junker twisting down in a spiral of black smoke or thousands of grey prisoners coming in holding up white flags.

The black and whiteness emphasised the nature of the struggle. Earlier conflicts with their red uniforms, flags and horses were painterly pageants by comparison. We were fighting the forces of darkness and the fact that so much of the conflict took place in the snows of Russia and northern Europe gave the black and white contrast greater symbolic impact. How could Auschwitz ever be in colour?

There was one exception in my monochromatic world. The London Blitz was a nightly firework display, full of bursting stars, tracer bullets and huge flares. The white beams of searchlights swept across the sky like giant scissors lighting up the silver satin lobes of barrage balloons. Blue and purple flares hung in the blackness like jellyfish at the top of a huge aquarium. The horizon was suffused with a soft orange glow as London's docks blazed in the far distance. My father woke me up to see the spectacular forest of light in the night sky. "It's the last night of the Blitz," he informed me. Later I wondered how he knew, but at the time I accepted it as I accepted all statements made by grown-ups. They always knew what was happening.

8. Necessary Fictions

On Saturday mornings before eight o'clock the four of us were despatched to Lakins the greengrocers to queue for vegetables. We had become a group - John Brown with his curly hair and red cheeks, the eldest by a few months and our natural leader, John Martin rather sallow and strained, Brian the youngest with an infectious laugh and me the tallest.

We set off at half-past seven in the morning when it was still dark, clutching the lists our mothers had supplied and wearing knitted balaclava helmets and gloves tied on a tape that went up one sleeve of our coats and down the other. When it snowed we dragged a homemade sled on which to load our purchases.

Outside the shuttered greengrocers there was already a forlorn-looking line of women with raw, windswept faces bundled up in headscarves, gloves and winter boots. As there was half an hour to wait before the shop opened, we employed the time pushing one another and reading comics that we bought at Farquarsons the newsagent next door. The headscarves made disparaging remarks about our behaviour.

"It's kids like this who are going to grow up and run the country."

"They're allowed to do what they like."

"I blame the parents."

"We never behaved like this."

"We'd've got a good hiding if we had."

"Sunny Stories" edited by Enid Blyton was our first encounter with the world of reading, a small pink-covered booklet with a riddle inside the front cover and a series of stories inside printed on grey wartime-standard paper that seemed to have small lumps of porridge embedded in it. But in spite of its dismal format, Enid Blyton was a magical writer for us and we became addicted to her tales of happy middle-class children exploring caves with lanterns by the seashore or discovering hoards of gold coins under the floorboards of country cottages.

From "Sunny Stories" we moved up to "The Dandy" with Korky the Cat on the cover. Our favourite was Desperate Dan, a cowboy with a stubbly chin eating enormous cow-pies with the tail hanging out of the pastry at one end in Cactusville, a town that combined stagecoaches, sheriffs and British policemen. The surrealistic humour of these comics was even more compelling than the fables of the Famous Five. In our puritanical and war-obsessed society the comics and radio offered a world of anarchic comedy, if not always politically correct. "The Beano" portrayed a piccaninny eating a melon on the front cover; another favourite character was Keyhole Kate, a noxious little girl with plaits, obsessed with peering through keyholes. Then there was Lord Snooty, an upper-class hero in a silk top-hat offering undisputed leadership to his working-class pals. The war itself became an extravaganza with Musso the Wop ('he's a big-a-da-flop') and ITMA, the high-voltage radio programme that we listened to compulsively every week, where Funf the German Spy whispered "Funf Speaking", a catch-phrase that became as compulsive as the charlady Mrs Mopp's "Can I Do Yer Now Sir?" or Colonel Chinstrap's fruity "I Don't Mind if I Do". It was a British surrealism that stood the war on its head, making fun of our own institutions, although it was ultimately patriotic. It linked back to the music hall and McGill's ribald seaside-postcards and forward to Spike Milligan and Monty Python. And to us queuing outside Lakins at half-past seven in the bleak winter half-light, it was life itself.

We were fiercely loyal in our comic-choices, rarely sharing them. Brian and I were devotees of "The Dandy" and John Brown and Martin "The Beano". From "The Beano" and "Dandy" we graduated to the "Hotspur", "Wizard" and "Champion", with their densely-packed columns of writing that required considerable reading ability to follow the weekly exploits of record-breaking athletes, acrobatic fighter-pilots and murderous commando-raids. Here was hyperbole of a different order, intensely male and more closely linked with the war, lacking the anarchist humour of "The Dandy" and its rivals. The serials and such features as "The Walkie-talkie Warrior" celebrated militarism and heroic daring-do reinforced by nuggets of information at the top of each page: "A convict who had been convicted 27 times won the V.C." followed by the surprising information that "The V.C. can be won by a woman" and "The

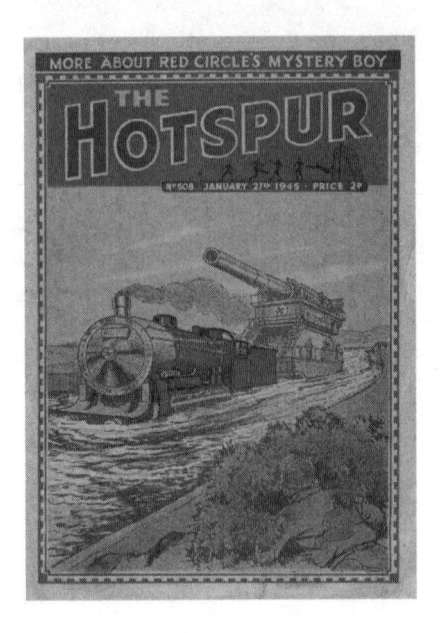

V.C is now made from German equipment captured in the last war". There were advertisements for packets of stamps and reconditioned shoes for which no coupons were necessary but the long war-narratives were, in Wallace Steven's phrase, necessary fictions as we waited in the freezing cold until, at long last, Mr Lakin emerged holding a long pole with a hook at one end which he hooked into the black shutters and rattled up.

The interior of the Lakin shop did not appear at first sight to be worth the wait. It consisted of a series of wooden partitions on the right-hand side which housed a narrow range of vegetables that looked as if they had just been hacked out of the frozen earth - soil-clogged King Edward potatoes, frostbitten Brussels sprouts the size of marbles and disfigured, grotesque parsnips. Large clods of mud clung to the produce which was nothing if not organic. Mrs Lakin, a fierce woman armed with a brass scoop in her knitted fingerless gloves, burrowed into the piles of potatoes and hurled them into our shopping bags. The only colours in the shop were the pre-war posters pinned to the walls or hanging banner-like from the ceiling advertising Cape apples and Jaffa bananas with brown-faced, white-teethed laughing women in spotted turbans holding up bunches of fruit we had never seen and never expected to see. The only real fruit on offer were sticks of unpleasant-looking pinkish rhubarb and apples of a hard green variety.

It was a green apple that I decided to steal as I stood in line for my potatoes and parsnips. It was my first public, deliberately criminal act and I am not sure why I attempted it. Perhaps it was simply experimental. I sneaked it from the pile as I was leaving the shop, fled down the alley behind the Kings Road, and bit into its sour flesh before hurling it high over a garden fence to destroy all evidence of my crime. But throwing the apple back was easier done than said. My crime would not disappear. I had still stolen the apple and I realised what it felt like to be an outcast from society. Guilt about the theft and a fear of being caught continued to haunt me. I had crossed some dreaded Rubicon that divided law-abiding people from pariah-like outcasts such as I had become. I experienced a physical sense of alienation that was impossible to expunge, on top of which there was no doubt in my mind that Lakin would take the necessary steps to track me down. Retribution was inevitable; there was no way I could wind the film back and for several months after my apple-stealing I was haunted by the fear of sudden arrest. Whenever I spotted a policeman walking towards me I crossed the road and vanished down a side street. Revisiting Lakins for the Saturday morning shop became an unnerving experience. I kept my head down and muttered my requests for frozen parsnips in a disguised voice. Gradually the realization that I had successfully accomplished a crime and escaped the punishment of society dawned on me but this did not alleviate my guilt at having committed it. I was branded with a scar of transgression and the stigma would not disappear although it grew less vivid with time.

Strangely enough this guilt did not extend to stealing apples from the Bulls' back garden three doors away from us. We clambered over the fence one afternoon to pick the unripe apple crop which was even harder and greener than that in Lakins. Scrumping was legitimate and sanctioned by tradition; or perhaps my violent vomiting and the spectacle of bright green apple-skins floating in a basin as I lay prostrate and retching until my chest ached, struck me as punishment enough.

After Lakins each Saturday we stopped at Pheasants the bakers, where Brian's mother, Lena, gave us uncooked crumpets which we ate with enormous enjoyment. Then we reported back to our respective homes for our change to be carefully checked against the pencilled list of prices before setting out again to the Odeon, where the Saturday Morning Pictures were about to start.

This was the high point of our Saturday mornings and our week. The Odeon was one of Rayners Lane's architectural triumphs, a splendid building with a vast auditorium and a background of ever-changing satin curtains looped in swags of purple and rose and orange. We drummed our shoes against the seats in front, hurled paper-darts into the projector-beam and sucked on sherbet packets through a liquorice tube. It was unalloyed delight. The manager, a large man with bryllcreemed hair and a double-breasted suit appeared on the stage in the spotlight holding a microphone and asked us if we were happy. "Yes!" we shrieked hurling another forest of paper darts and drumming our feet continuously. Apparently not satisfied with our level of response, he repeated his question, exciting us into a frenzy of acclamation which only died down when the curtains swung open to display the Saturday Morning Song which we sang following a ball bouncing along the top of the words on the screen.

The films began, short black-and-white movies mostly from America. My favourite was Hopalong Cassidy, a cowboy encased in black leather with silver trappings who seemed infinitely more glamorous than the Lone Ranger with his guitar on his too-shiny horse, Trigger. The Three Stooges lounging around on street corners in Brooklyn wearing reversed caps and speaking an almost incomprehensible American urban dialect were nevertheless as acceptable as if we saw them in Rayners Lane. Abbott and Costello in the Foreign Legion, waddling about with guns and handkerchiefs under their caps in imitation of Beau Geste, were one of the high points of film-comedy as far as we were concerned, funnier than Laurel and Hardy. But no one was

as hilarious as Will Hay, the teacher in gown and mortar-board outsmarted by his pupils or as the stationmaster assisted by Fatty Arbuckle growing cucumbers across the railway tracks. The final offering was always a serial, ending with a desperate moment when the ceiling slowly descended on the hero in a windowless room or he gradually lost his grip on the steel girder of the bridge in the path of an oncoming train. We came out of the Odeon emotionally exhausted by these spectacles although the episode the following week was inevitably an anticlimax: a concealed trapdoor in the floor enabled the hero to escape or he leapt safely on to the roof of the train.

The magic of the Saturday morning flicks never failed. It was America's greatest export to us, supplemented with occasional feature films – "The Scarlet Pimpernel" starring Leslie Howard as the English spy in the years of the French Revolution who had us shouting "Zounds!" and running around with curtains round our necks for a week afterwards and "Black Swan" with Tyrone Power, a pirate-epic in fantastic colour, bursting with red cannon-fire and dazzling blue seas, the first technicolor film we saw. The Saturday Morning cinema was never about the war but occasionally we went to a feature film that had been advertised as exciting. "In Which We Serve" earned a grudging visit but turned out to be boring with airmen in lifeboats bobbing up and down on the black Atlantic waves. Other grown-up films that we were occasionally trapped into seeing always seem to show a man opposite a woman at a round restaurant table with a lamp in the centre talking earnestly for hours while they held hands.

American comics completed our cultural fare although they were disliked by teachers and parents. They were our introduction to the war in the Pacific which was unknown and far distant. Terry and the Pirates appeared in bright green uniforms hacking through impenetrable jungle which concealed yellow-faced men with fearsome swords and their teeth sticking out. Dick Tracey with his crackling, lightning-style wristwatch radio seemed to embody the future as English comics never did. Superman hurtled among the skyscrapers and scooped up criminals with exploding streaks of white light that careered across the differently-shaped frames of the comic in a way that never happened in "The Beano" or "The Dandy" and we had to learn a different visual language as strange as the U.S. servicemen who had started to arrive, handing out flat packets of chewing-gum as they came out of the Underground in response to the mantra, "Got any gum chum?"

American comics were impossible to buy and acquired rarity status in addition to the immense prestige of being disapproved of by grownups. They circulated clandestinely, luridly coloured and often with an erotic content. One I saw depicted a curvaceous woman hanging by her wrists from a roof-beam while three men in striped suits and trilby hats stood around her. Her clinging dress had been ripped open revealing her breasts and one of the men was holding a long whip. Another held a glowing cigarette against her nipple while he questioned her. It was clearly extraordinary territory and we crowded around, staring at the vivid images as if our future depended on them, as perhaps it did.

9 Love and Lust

Victorine - Mrs Smart as I called her - was our neighbour on one side. "Geev eem to me," she would say, "'e is my sweet'eart!" Nobody else called me her sweetheart. My mother thankfully handed me over. Mrs Smart had bright red cheeks like apples and plump arms with dimples at the elbows and an apron with flowers to which she clasped me.

"'E is my darling," she said, giving me a hug.

"Victorine is Belgian," Mum explained, as if that accounted for her irrational display of enthusiasm. "She escaped from Liege during the First World War in a sack." The sack intrigued me. What kind of sack was it? Was she loaded on to a ship like a sack at the docks? Was the sack thrown on to a cart pulled by a horse past the German lines?

Mrs Smart took me inside her house which although next door, was another country. There was a large leather sofa pinned by metal buttons with crocheted lace doilies draped over the back and two oval, sepia photographs in deep mahogany frames on either side of an upright piano with candlestick holders. She had two boys, one grown-up who had done something wrong – married a woman his parents didn't like or not married her, I was uncertain which. Now he was in the army wearing a uniform buttoned to the neck and a forage cap, in the oval frame, brown with clouded edges as if he were going to float away. He was called Laurie, which seemed a strange name for a boy. Perhaps it was Belgian and perhaps Mrs Smart had come to England in a sack loaded on to a barge because she gave me a wooden barge with a dark red triangular sail that I sailed in the bath. One day, she said, she hoped to see her two sisters again. They had been left behind in Liège. "After thees terrible war," she said. Everything was always after this war.

"We bought thees 'ouse because we saw thees two young men digging in the garden next door and I said to Lionel, "They look like nice young men. We must buy the 'ouse."

The two young men were my father and Uncle Norman. Dad liked Mrs Smart a lot and called her Vicky. Mum said she could always tell foreigners because they waved their hands about but Dad waved his hands about too. He said perhaps it was because he had grown up in the East End where there were a lot of Poles and Armenians who waved their hands about. Dad was dark-skinned with black, shining hair that he combed back in imitation of Georges Carpentier, a French boxer who had been popular when he was in his twenties. Some people thought Dad was Italian but he had never been abroad, although he said he would when the war was over. He liked foreign things including wine although there was no wine in Rayners Lane during the war. I had never seen a bottle of wine.

"I can get you half a dozen bottles," Mr Smart said to Dad over the garden fence. Lionel Smart was a butcher in Finsbury Park and claimed he could get anything. He had a shining bald head that looked as if it has been polished with lard and short plump fingers like sausages.

"Anything you want," he insisted, "just name it. Wine, beef, a crate of whiskey, nice leg of lamb."

My father wasn't interested in Mr Smart's proposals but Mum was. She saw it as a way of supplementing the meagre rations.

"It's all right for you," she said to Dad when he objected to Mr Smart's offers, "you don't have to queue two hours for a pair of kippers." My mother hated all the queuing she had to do. If she heard from a neighbour that kippers or liver or rabbit, which were off the ration, had suddenly appeared, she rushed to the bus-stop and waited in a queue outside the shop for two hours. Then she queued for the bus to bring her home again. Sometimes it took nearly all day to buy a pair of kippers. But Mrs Smart never queued and the Smarts had all the food luxuries they wanted. Dad was still against Mr Smart's offers. "We don't want any dealings with the black market," he said. I didn't know what the black market was exactly but there was a lot of talk about it and it sounded exciting. I imagined it might be like the market opposite South Harrow Underground station which was built under the railway arches and was always so dark the lights were switched on during the day. Once Mum bought me a clay pipe from a stall in the market to blow soap bubbles, but I dropped it, so we went back and bought another and I dropped that too so we went back and bought a third. But the real Black Market was everywhere: there were posters telling us not to use it because the merchant seamen were risking their lives to bring food in convoys across the Atlantic while the U-boats were attacking every week. Dad explained that the Black Market meant that people with money could buy extra goods, but rationing ensured that we all had the same, which was fair.

"It's all right for you," Mum said again, "you don't have to do the shopping." Then she added, "You don't know half the things I do. Sometimes I run up a dress for coupons instead of cash so we can have something extra." Mr Smart talked to Dad about things falling off the back of a lorry and I imagined parcels bouncing along the grass-verge by the road as the lorry rattled along.

One day Mrs Smart said, "We're thinking of moving."

Nobody else moved during the war except the Smarts. "He can fiddle anything," my mother said. I had never heard of anyone moving before and I didn't want Mrs Smart to go because I was her sweetheart and she was mine, but suddenly she had gone.

After a few months we visited the Smarts in their new flat which was on the first floor and had windows with diamond-shaped panes of glass. We travelled to Cockfosters, the last station on the Piccadilly Line and I counted twenty-nine stations; Mr Smart met us in his new car. "I'd like to know how he gets the petrol," Mum said. "I shouldn't ask if I were you."

One afternoon my mother and I were visiting Mrs Smart and having dinner when the Alert siren started to wail. I ran downstairs to look out of the door up at the sky. There was a doodlebug, the first I have seen, a black, pilotless rocket gliding silently across the sky, flames spurting out of the black cylinder mounted on top of the fuselage like something from another planet. We crouched down in the bend of the stairs because Mrs Smart said that was the safest place to be; she held my head tightly under her arm and I heard her heart thumping while I listened to the engine. There were three deep thumps before the engine cut out. I counted up to ten because I knew it took that time to explode. Later I heard it had blown up over Amersham and killed ten people.

The doodlebugs were more frightening than the V2s which came soon after because the V2s were giant rockets that struck without warning. We couldn't see or hear them and the first we knew about them was that a street of houses had been destroyed.

A few months after the doodlebug I was with Mrs Smart listening to the one o'clock news when it was announced that Paris had been liberated and the Free French and American troops were entering the city. The Marseillaise was playing. Mrs Smart stretched across the table and held my hand. Tears were pouring down her cheeks as she dabbed at her eyes with her lace handkerchief. "Isn't it wonderful?" she said. "It's going to end. This dreadful war is going to end. Now I can see my sisters. I thought I'd never see them again."

For the first time I realised what the war meant to those in Europe.

The neighbour on the other side was Mrs Bridges, a large lady who walked with a swing of her hips that we found irresistibly amusing. At first she was on good terms with my mother and asked her to make dresses and petticoats from parachute silk which was available without coupons.

My mother had begun dressmaking for women in Rayners Lane and was developing a small business although she refused to regard it as such. She insisted that she didn't go out to work as the other mothers did. "It's a hobby," she maintained. "I enjoy doing it. Of course the money comes in useful. But it isn't much." This was true, particularly as she adjusted her prices according to what she thought the customers could pay. It meant that most paid no more than two pounds for a dress and a shilling to have a hem turned up. "It's all they can afford in Rayners Lane," she said.

My mother loved her dressmaking and said repeatedly she would sooner cut out a dress than do housework. In spite of her declared amateurism, she was professional in her approach. Every afternoon at two o'clock she went up to the small front bedroom where there was an ancient Singer sewing machine with a foot-treadle and a large cutting-out table my father had constructed and there she worked until six. She kept an appointments book in which she wrote down all her orders and prices and the customers' measurements. Her business expanded over the years without advertising. She was obviously a good dressmaker although she never viewed it as having any social status or as being as prestigious as the job of a typist or telephonist.

She fitted her customers in the front-room and I was strictly forbidden to play in the vicinity. One afternoon I wandered around to the front bay window where the curtains were drawn and discovered that by pulling myself up by the windowsill and standing on the edge of the concrete surround where it joined the brickwork, I could peer through a crack in the curtains and see Mrs Bridges without her clothes on. Mrs Bridges was a large, curvaceous lady, who had stripped down to a pink, multi-strapped and boned corset with suspenders holding up her stockings and cups full of her overflowing breasts. I clung breathless with excitement but the exertion of hanging on to the windowsill was considerable and I dropped to the path after a few minutes before clambering back up again. Mrs Bridges had moved around and had her arms raised in the air while my mother knelt in front of her with a tape-measure and her mouth full of pins. I felt my heart beating furiously as she swung around displaying her shining corset to my view, looking straight towards me. I realised this spectacle was connected with sex, but was unsure what that was all about. John Brown had stated categorically that babies came out of women's stomachs, a plausible explanation and one I accepted as superior to fables about storks and gooseberry bushes. On the other hand, Brian Hartel's assertion that babies were ordered and collected from the hospital seemed equally probable. John Brown claimed that a man put his tool into the woman to make a baby but this seemed too ridiculous to be true. John Brown said a lot of silly things and this was clearly one of them. Yet his obsessive interest in tits and bums was obviously connected with Mrs Bridges' anatomy and here I was in the front seat of the show. Mrs Bridges' large breasts were bulging out of her shining pink corset. The two shining globes of her buttocks were displayed as she moved around to allow my mother to take her measurements. I held on as long as I could, squinting through the gap in the curtains.

Mrs Bridges' endowments were the topic of conversation when we met in the alley. We took to goading her, following her at a distance imitating the swings of her anatomy until she turned round, when we dived into the nearest gateway. We christened her Jumbo, following her down the street, giggling and pushing one another until she stopped and looked behind her.

One afternoon disaster struck. She abruptly turned around and marched back to the front door of my house, rang the bell and spoke to my mother while we watched from a distance. "You're for it now," my friends said, melting away. And in the evening I was confronted with my behaviour.

"Mrs Bridges says you've been laughing at her," my father said accusingly.

I denied it. I claimed we had been laughing at each other and she just happened to overhear us.

"She says you've been following her along the street."

I denied it again and started to believe my own story becoming more inventive as I did so. I explained that we had been playing a game called shadows where we stamped on each other's shadows and this had resulted in Mrs Bridges' mistaken belief that we had been making fun of her. I implied she was a victim of her own paranoia and that we were blameless. It occurred to me that Mrs Bridges might have glimpsed me spying on her through the curtains and I become even more insistent on my version of events. My explanation was grudgingly accepted and I was let off with a warning.

The upshot was that the unfortunate Mrs Bridges felt even more persecuted and snubbed my mother whenever she passed her, a treatment that my mother found painful especially from the next-door neighbour. If Mum had been able to move she would have done so but it was impossible. She was stuck with the oppressive presence of Mrs Bridges who made her hostility felt every day on every possible occasion. I felt guilty for the lies I had told but the feud now had a momentum of its own and it was too late I told myself, for me to do anything about it.

Mrs Bridges continued to inspire my erotic fantasies however. I followed her in my imagination, undressing in her gleaming corset in our front room until the scene became part of that stock of fantasies that males, young and old, carry around inside their heads.

10 Our Finest Hour

We had just finished listening to Mr Churchill on the wireless.

Dad wasn't so sure about Churchill. "He says, 'though the Empire lasts a thousand years, men will still say, this was their finest hour', but it isn't going to last a thousand years. Look at India. India has to have its independence after the war."

"I don't like that Gandhi," Mum said. "You'd think he'd wear a proper suit to come and see the Prime Minister, not that nasty old robe."

"It doesn't matter what he wears."

"Yes it does. He's all skin and bone."

"He wants to dress the same as poor people."

"You'd think someone would lend him a suit to come to England."

Mum was an Imp when she was growing up in Kelvedon. It was the junior branch of the Conservatives. Imp stood for Imperialist.

"Churchill's no friend of the working man," Dad said.

"Of course he isn't, he's a Marlborough."

Dad wasn't sure who the Marlboroughs were but Mum was.

"He's a descendant of John, Duke of Marlborough who won the Battle of Blenheim. That's why they built Blenheim Palace. Churchill was born there and proposed to his wife, Clementine, in the gardens."

There was a Blenheim aeroplane in my cigarette card collection. It was a small bomber with a long cockpit and yellow wings.

"He loves fighting," my mother said, biting off the darning thread.

"I know," Dad said.

I hadn't been able to follow Churchill's speech very easily because there were long gaps between the phrases so by the time he started one I had forgotten what the last one was. It was like slipping about on ice, trying to jump from one phrase to the next.

"War's in his blood," Mum informed us. "He wants to be like his ancestor, the duke."

Dad mentioned the siege of Sidney Street where Churchill was in charge and people were killed but Mum ignored him.

"His mother, Jenny, was a rich American," she said, pushing her hand up into the sock and twisting it round to see how well she had darned it. "That's how he got America to join the war." Mum liked Churchill's mother even though she was American. "The American heiresses wanted to marry into our aristocracy. We had the titles and they had the money."

"They always get together," Dad said.

After Churchill's speech, Dad started writing to his brother Norman, who had been sent to India as manager of British Oxygen in Calcutta. I missed him because it was always exciting when he came to see us. The letters we received were very small, photographed on special paper so they didn't take up much space in the plane.

When Dad wrote a letter it was an elaborate performance. We had to be quiet. He commandeered the whole dining-room table and laid out his writing paper, the pen with a special nib, a bottle of blue-black ink and a large sheet of blotting paper. He always wrote a first draft and then copied it out in his sloping copperplate handwriting, with thin and thick strokes and curly flourishes on the capital letters. It looked very elegant, especially the capital D's and G's which were like swans' necks, bowing their heads in the water. It was very different from Mum's handwriting which was round and quick. Dad had written the first draft and was copying it out, checking the spelling.

"How do you spell *necessary*?" he asked Mum.

"One C and two Ss."

"How do you spell *until*?"

"One l. How is it I can spell and you can't?"

"I don't know. Does *margarine* have an *a* or an *e* in the middle?"

"It's because I stayed on at school until I was sixteen and you left at fourteen."

Then the bomb fell.

There was a deep, violent thump and the dining table rose up into the air and half turned, coming down on its side. The bottle of ink shot up towards the ceiling and emptied its contents on the wallpaper, running in black rivulets down the oatmeal surface. The pens and blotting paper and first draft skittered across the room. I was thrown to the floor and pulled Bob towards me putting my hands over his head. We were all on the floor.

"Bloody hell!"

I had never heard my father swear so vehemently before.

We lay on the floor waiting for the next crash but there wasn't one. I didn't know what to do except cover my head and listen to the ink dripping over the edge of the table. I looked up and saw the ink running down the wallpaper on to the carpet. I was trembling but stayed on the floor until I heard whistles and a violent banging on the front door and a voice shouting through the letter-box telling us to stay indoors. I could only think that Dad's letter had been ruined and there was ink staining the carpet. Slowly we got to our feet and begin to clear up the mess. Mum was upset about the ink and started sponging the carpet with a basin of water. After a while an ARP man came to the house again and said, "Jerry didn't want to take them back. He just unloaded them." Later we were told that a stick of five bombs had been dropped in a line across Rayners Lane and Ruislip.

In the morning I went to look at the house that had been hit in Capthorne Avenue on the other side of the Kings Road. The front wall was ripped away, and I could see inside as though I was looking in an open doll's house. The bed was tilted at an angle and a chest of drawers had slid across the room and looked as if it was about to fall. Nobody had been killed but the boy who lived there came to school next day in his sister's cardigan, buttoned up the wrong side and we laughed at him.

The war was coming closer. A week after the bomb dropped I heard Hitler's voice on the wireless, a violent, hysterical screeching. He was giving one of his speeches and the crowd roared their approval. It was the first time I had heard another language and the German words sounded strange and terrifying like barbed wire. Hitler's voice rose to a crescendo and I suddenly imagined he was next-door and about to burst with his troops through the wall. I ran out of the room, terrified. "It's only the wireless," Dad said, but that didn't make me feel any better. The sound of Hitler's voice was more real than his photographs. I was more scared than I had been when the bomb dropped.

The wireless was more real than any other form of communication.

"This is the six o' clock news, with Alvar Liddell reading it" became the comforting mantra of the BBC news that we listened to every night. We never questioned the truthfulness of the BBC or whether any news-items was censored. Occasionally we would hear Lord Haw-Haw broadcasting from Berlin telling us stories of British ships sunk at sea and towns bombed, but we didn't believe his stories which were dismissed as Nazi propaganda, even though we knew some of them – such as the continual raids on Ipswich where my grandparents lived, were true. Lord Haw-Haw was the nickname of William Joyce that made him seem like a comic character out of "The Beano". Later I learned he was an Ulsterman, a violent anti-Semite and a dedicated Nazi who was executed after the war although he had taken official German citizenship in 1939.

Throughout the war the BBC was our guardian, guide and friend. The Royal Family addressed us in their strange voices at Christmas and other great events. Government officials lectured us in stern accents on what to eat and how to cook it. The Radio Doctor Charles Hill persuaded us in avuncular tones to keep as fit and bouncy as he was. The Brain's Trust with Dr Joad intoning, "It depends what you mean by…" was surprisingly popular and I listened to it before I could understand either the questions or the answers. Vera Lynn and Gracie Fields sang "We'll Meet Again, Sometime, Somewhere", "Sally" and Al Bowlly's "Goodbye Sweetheart" which became national anthems of the war. "Workers' Playtime" was designed to speed up production in the munitions factories and "Children's Hour", one of the few programmes I actively disliked, signed off every evening with Uncle Mac's "Goodnight children, everywhere."

But the most important function of the wireless for us was that like our comics, it offered uproarious satire. ITMA, "It's That Man Again," which originally referred to Hitler but came to stand for the comedian Tommy Handley himself brought popular, demotic speech into our homes in contrast to the ponderous upper class voices of the establishment. We repeated the catchphrases endlessly and the acronyms that parodied the new fashion for initials in government administration (TTFN – ta-ta for now) or the spread of government bureaucracy such as The Ministry of Aggravation and Mysteries at the Office of Twerps. ITMA was only one of a series of radio programmes in the long parade of British comedy which included Gert and Daisy, the subversive Cockney girls with their working-class, female perspective on society, Arthur Askey and Richard "Stinker" Murdoch in "Bandwagon," another high-speed show that undermined pomposity with its "Hullo Playmates" and a stream of comedians from the music-halls– Sandy Powell ("Can You Hear me, Mother"?), Cyril Fletcher with his doggerel rhymes and Murgatroyd and Winterbottom in "Much Binding in the Marsh" with their pattering lyrics that summed up the week's news at the end of each programme. And there were the Western Brothers that I particularly enjoyed with their parody of cawing upper-class accents that were not so dissimilar to the Oxford accents of the BBC commentators.

How one spoke was clearly important, although parents and teachers in Rayners Lane only touched the edge of the English obsession. I was aware that Uncle Norman spoke differently from my father even though they were brothers and had grown up in Bow together. I was aware that Uncle Norman pronounced "coupon" and "restaurant" with a nasal intonation at the end of the words whereas my father sounded the final consonants. "All educated people speak the same way," Uncle Norman explained to me, and I decided that I too would honk at the end of words like coupon because I wanted to sound educated.

There was occasionally talk of girls who took elocution lessons to speak English properly, but it was never suggested that we should take any. My parents made occasional sorties into pronunciation emphasising that there were definite rules. "H"s were never to be dropped and "t"s were always to be sounded; as I habitually referred to Brian Hartel with a dropped "h" at the beginning and a dropped "t" in the middle, I was attacked twice for my pronunciation in the same word. There was a total ban on "ain't" and "wotcha!" our greeting to one another, was regarded as vulgar although I discovered later that it was a contraction of "What cheer?" the Elizabethan greeting that opens "The Tempest". A teacher at school explained that the "h" in "whale" should always be pronounced, an eccentricity that greatly amused us. Otherwise we were left alone. Churchill seemed to have his own growling intonation which was different from that of the announcers and other politicians. He pronounced some words with a particular emphasis of his own as when he said "Nassy" instead of "Nazi" but I had decided by this time that I didn't want to imitate Churchill.

11 Pyrrhic Victory

Much of the time the war did not affect us directly. We were not Channel Islanders with the Gestapo standing on every street corner and after the Blitz there was a three-year lull before civilians were attacked from the air again. But the war continued to affect us in subtle ways. I got up at six in the morning to see my father, since otherwise I should never have seen him except at weekends; he was working a sixty-hour week and arrived home at eight in the evening after I had been sent to bed. Being up, I volunteered to cook his breakfast which invariably consisted of a fried egg, two fried rashers of back bacon, a slice of fried bread with fried tomatoes or fried potatoes and occasionally fried mushrooms.

This fry-up was not as straightforward as it seemed and frequently resulted in disaster. First of all the egg has to be cracked into a glass tumbler and held up to inspect for purity. I never discovered a bad egg; we were registered for eggs with Mrs Henderson, four doors along Capthorne Avenue; the eggs from her ducks and chickens, which walked about in the kitchen, were invariably fresh. But the inspection had to be made; I cracked the egg, a tricky feat as my fingers were not long enough to hold the egg securely and it was often a leathery-shelled duck-egg which bounced back unbroken or slipped out of my fingers on to the black-and-white tiles of the kitchen floor. But if the inspection was successful, I prepared the frying pan. This battered utensil was never cleaned out and the layer of fat in it appeared to be as ancient as the pan itself which had been transported from Bow in the 1930's. If yet more fat was needed, I added a lump of dripping prised from the basin holding the residue from the Sunday joint. This precious substance contained a rich brown jelly concealed at the bottom of the basin like a hidden treasure. I was careful not to disturb this jelly because it was an exotic gastronomic treat, spread on bread with a sprinkling of salt. The fat in the pan, I waited until it was sizzling and when I judged it to be at the correct temperature, dropped in two rashers of back bacon which immediately went into convulsions, hunching their rinds up and down like the Loch Ness monster. I was required to snip these so they lay flat, a tricky operation because the rinds were thick and the sizzling fat sprayed burning globules on to my wrist. I then added tomatoes; mushrooms were an expensive rarity and only occurred once or twice a year.

But there was always fried bread, an item that drew on all my culinary skills, for my father insisted on the exactly the right shade of amber, neither smoking black which happened if the fat had over-heated, nor white and sponge-like if I dropped it in too soon. Next came the egg, the most challenging of all. I poured it slowly from the tumbler into the hissing fat, splashed the yolk with a teaspoon until it reached the required shade of orange and then removed it from the pan by sliding the slice underneath and lifting it towards the waiting bread. As there was so much fat in the pan, the egg was liable to skate around as though on an ice-rink and on several disastrous occasions it slid off the slice, disappearing into the space between the cooker and the wall. But when I did manage to manoeuvre the egg on to the plate the whole *oeuvre* had to be arranged attractively and served simultaneously with a cup of tea that has its own strict rules of engagement - the pot taken to the kettle, the three minute wait for it to brew, the milk poured into the cup before the tea and not after.

My failure rate was high but every so often I produced a breakfast that earned my father's commendation. "Well done!" he'd say. I felt a surge of culinary pride and we'd talk about matters of the moment prompted by the headlines of *The Daily Express* which has been pushed through the letterbox while I was dealing with the egg and fried bread. Every morning we played a game of trying to guess what the headlines would be before I opened the paper. There was the progress of the Eighth Army through North Africa, the Burma campaign with the Chindits and the invasion of Sicily. Sometimes the headlines got stuck as they did with the battle for Monte Cassino. The monastery on a high hill blocked the allies' advance up Italy to Rome. It was the most important monastery in Europe but the Flying Fortresses bombed it continuously while the German paratroopers dug into the mountain and became impossible to drive out. The allies landed at Anzio north of the monastery but the Germans bottled up the troops who came ashore there. The headlines in *"The Daily Express"* were about Monte Cassino week after week as the allies tried to capture it and the German paratroopers under General Kesselring hung on. The monastery was shelled into oblivion and the Italian refugees from the town who sheltered there were all killed. The Americans attacked it over the river then the New Zealanders, the Gurkhas, the British Eighth army and the Poles. There were four battles and it was six months before the allies captured the hill and by then there was nothing left of the monastery except piles of stones. "It wasn't worth it," everybody said.

When Dad had gone to work there was still another hour before my mother got up. I made jigsaw puzzles, sticking pictures of Hurricanes winging through blue skies or Lancasters on night bombing-raids on to plywood and cutting out the pieces with a fretsaw attached to a large motor. The fretsaw produced a loud clattering noise like a Lancaster taking off and taxied across the kitchen floor but I steered the plywood around the blade in jigsaw shapes and managed to avoid sawing my thumbs off. Making jigsaws rather than solving them became an obsession.

One morning, as a temporary respite from the manufacture of jigsaws, I entered a painting competition in my mother's "Daily Graphic". The wartime quality of the newsprint made the colours run into each other like blotting paper but I posted my entry, a windmill in a field full of tulips, to the newspaper. A week later I received a prize: a large hardback book of animals that leapt up as the book was opened - lions, zebras, elephants and camels. It was my first prize and the first book I had seen where the pictures stood up.

Dad devoted Sunday evenings to playing games with me. We played billiards, shove ha'penny, draughts, darts and finally chess. Billiards was the best but had a limited life. We acquired a half-size billiard table, which was too long and too wide for our front room, a substantial Edwardian piece of furniture with turned mahogany legs and an emerald green cloth over a slate bed. The ends of the cues banged into the wall producing a white line of plaster against the wallpaper that my mother objected to. As we also had to stand on the sofa at one end, there was very little space left for my mother who complained that there was no point in having a front room if there was nowhere to sit down. The billiard-table had to go, but it was a sad loss. I never forgot the delight of coming down in the morning and practising alone on the green expanse of felt with the luxury of its trappings, the inlaid cues and the brass and mahogany scoreboard.

The inferior shove ha'penny board took its place but it was not in the same league as the billiards table and I never acquired the same affection for it nor the finesse to shove the ha'pennies into their respective beds. Dad was skilful and won nearly every game. Draughts was even more of a catastrophe for me. I lost continuously, Dad leapfrogging his king backwards and forwards across the board, leaving my pieces decimated, and laughing as he did so. My blood boiled at this injustice and I was close to tears.

"Any fool can win," he'd say, "it's losing that's difficult."

This was cold comfort for me. What was the point of playing if you didn't win? I tried to pretend that winning or losing were a matter of indifference, but without success. Winning was what it was all about. The competition was heightened by our games of darts. We played 301, Round the Clock, and Cricket nearly all of which my father won. He was particularly skilful at hitting double 19 and finishing on that number, with the accompanying laughter that made me want to hurl my remaining dart into his back and run out of the room.

It was only later with chess that the tables finally turned and I gradually began to win, exacting revenge for my years of defeat at billiards, shove ha'penny, draughts and darts. But our Sunday evening games together were coming to an end. And my father's laugh was still there, win or lose, in defeat as in triumph. I was left with a pyrrhic victory, the Oedipal contest that can never be won.

12 Uncle Joe and the Neighbours

We sometimes called middle-aged men uncle even though they were not members of the family, so it was not unusual when Josef Stalin was presented to us as Uncle Joe, the avuncular gentleman who wanted our salvage. The fact that he had executed dozens of his own generals who had the misfortune to lose a battle and connived with Hitler in the mass murder of 15,000 Polish intellectuals in a forest near Smolensk in 1940 was effectively concealed from us. Uncle Joe's beaming face with its handlebar moustache shone down from scarlet banners decorated with the gold hammer and sickle. We were exhorted to collect salvage for the Sword of Stalingrad, a huge Excalibur-like shining silver sword that was to be presented to Uncle Joe by Churchill to commemorate the Russian victory of the Battle of Stalingrad.

For months we had seen the news photographs and films of white uniformed soldiers fighting in the snow, of partisans hanging from beams and of German tanks abandoned in snowdrifts. Every shop, basement, and street had been fought for. There were two million casualties before the Russian counter-attack led by Marshal Zhukhov defeated von Paulus.

Uncle Joe was a friend of Churchill and the saviour of the Russian people. Now the sword was being made by Wilkinsons and inscribed to the "steel-hearted citizens of Stalingrad" by King George the Sixth. Before Churchill presented it to Uncle Joe it would tour the country – Birmingham, Cardiff, Belfast, Coventry and London. It was a big event.

We pulled our trolley from house to house along Exeter and Torbay Road, banging on doors and demanding salvage for Uncle Joe with all the ideological righteousness that was our due. The residents did not have much to give. The spiked railings that swung from post to post outside the hedges had already been removed. We were lucky to receive a pile of *Everybodys*, a battered aluminium saucepan or a buckled bike wheel. One householder gave us a dartboard made of brown paper which we unrolled the length of Exeter Road into Widdecombe Crescent, amazed at how far it stretched. There were rumours of housewives being asked to contribute wedding rings, bracelets and necklaces but wisely they did not give them to us.

Collecting salvage for Uncle Joe merged into collecting bonfire materials for Guy Fawkes which we celebrated by burning Adolf Hitler on November 5th. The absence of fireworks did not spoil our enjoyment in the least. We dragged our guy around Rayners Lane asking for pennies and constructed a large pyre in the alley opposite John Brown's house, perilously close to the fences on either side. My mother contributed an Aunt Sally that she no longer needed, a large statuesque bust of stuffed canvas with no head or arms but breasts resembling the Venus de Milo which delighted John Brown. She was a magnificent guy. We decorated her female form with a Hitler mask and set fire to the pyre we had built; the blaze roared skyward with a high tunnel of flames and sparks; the wire squares of her lower half turned white-hot and we were besieged by neighbours threatening to call the fire brigade. We threw water on to the fences and as the flames subsided roasted potatoes in the embers and consumed their blackened cases with relish.

The Brown garden was the centre of our activities, halfway along the alley which ran between the back gardens of Capthorne Avenue and Lynton Road on one side and Kings Road on the other. The Brown gate was always open, jammed against the concrete of the alley, the lawn a flattened mud expanse where we met instinctively without making definite arrangements. Unlike other gardens the Brown garden was democratic territory and Mrs Brown, who had been to Grammar School - uniquely among our parents – did not care that we tramped in and out.

Beryl Brown was manifestly different. Her dining-room possessed a set of Dickens novels in blue leatherette binding with gold lettering and there was a carelessness about her domestic arrangements which bordered on the bohemian, heightened by the suspicion that her beds were never properly made or the furniture polished. The Browns possessed a telephone and Beryl phoned her friend Hilda Martin across the alley, a wanton extravagance that shocked my mother. She also wore a headscarf and slacks and smoked in the street and had taken up with Cobber, an Australian air-force sergeant who was in the kitchen every day, his blue tunic with three stripes hanging over the back of the chair. He and Beryl went on holiday to Cornwall together and held parties on Saturday nights where there was dancing and games of musical chairs. "Beryl doesn't care what anyone thinks," my mother said.

The Brown garage, set back from the alley with its peeling blue doors of corrugated metal served as our goal for football, each goal registering with a metallic crash as the tennis ball hit the metal. We peered through the crack in the doors at the Brown car, set up on blocks in the darkness, the only car in the alley and like Mr Brown out of circulation during the war. Cobber had taken his place. Ron Brown had been commissioned into the air force and appeared from time to time in his neatly-pressed officer's blue uniform. He was, the neighbours said, too good for Beryl who was no better than she should be.

I was sent over to the Browns when Mum and Dad went to the pictures on Saturday nights and slept on a mattress stuffed with straw that squeaked like mice whenever I turned over. The mattress smelled like a hayloft but Mrs Brown said it was healthy. What irritated my mother was that Dad enjoyed Beryl's company so much. He had found a job for her at Electroflo, the factory where he worked and they walked back together from the station every evening.

"I don't know what you see in her," Mum complained, "you wouldn't like it if I wore slacks. She doesn't even wear make-up and her frizzy hair's all over the place."

Dad said he didn't mind what she wore which only made matters worse. "All the men like Beryl," Mum confided to Lena Hartel.

Mrs Brown was a forceful mother. She shook John until his teeth chattered when she suspected him of telling lies. She had a directness of attack that was formidable and I stayed out of her way when she was on the warpath.

For us the chief attraction of the Brown garden was the tall silver birch that overhung the fence, the only tree in the alley. We climbed it, swung from its branches, collected catkins and peeled its bark in long strips. Every summer we built a tree-house dragging up planks and hammering them into the branches. We hauled up a square of old carpet, and comics and sat reading. No other garden could compete with the idyll of the tree house.

Certainly not the Martin's. Hilda Martin in her tight curls and striped nurse's uniform with wide waistband and watch pinned to her lapel was the antithesis of Beryl Brown, even though they were friends. She was always in a hurry and wouldn't allow us inside the house, although we occasionally ventured into the garden. John Martin's sister Anne had blonde, shining hair and I was half in love with her but she treated me with distain, copying her mother's manner. The youngest Martin, known as Podge trailed behind us in spite of numerous rejections. John Martin's chief claim to fame was that he has been fed on 120 bananas a day as a baby because of a life-threatening disease. As none of us had ever seen a banana this gave him considerable prestige. What his mysterious illness had been we never discovered but his skin retained a yellowish hue and I imagined the bananas had permanently coloured his skin from the inside.

Although we were never allowed inside the Martin house we knew that Mrs Martin entertained Jan, a Polish air force officer stationed at Northolt. Jan was quiet and dignified. We felt sorry for him because Poland had been invaded by the Nazis; the Free Polish Air Force flew from Northolt and I associated Jan with news-photographs I had seen of the Polish cavalry on horses charging against German tanks.

Mr Martin was away in the army. He had worked at Harrods before the war, "but only as a counter jumper" Mum said. I imagined him leaping backwards and forwards over the counter like a rabbit. "The Martins think they're somebody but they're nobody really," was my mother's verdict.

Brian Hartel lived towards the end of the alley in a house that was different from ours. It had a dining-room-cum-kitchen and the bathroom was downstairs. In the bathroom was a long line of golliwogs cut from Robinson's marmalade jars, pasted on the wall. Brian's mother was very house-proud. I was allowed into the kitchen but had to take off my shoes and leave them at the door. Their taps had red rubber extensions which hung down like cow's udders. Intrigued by these, I turned the taps on, squeezed the udders and squirted the spray around the sink managing to splash halfway up the wall. For this offence, I was banished from the house for several months.

The Hartel's back garden was like a Dig for Victory poster with lines of runner beans on criss-cross poles like wigwams, rows of lettuces, tomato plants bulging with fruit and, near the house, a cluster of tall hollyhocks that intrigued me with their violet and pink flowers and cushioned leaves. Bill Hartel worked for the Gas, Light and Coke Company and was, like my father, in a reserved occupation. He was very political and given to reading aloud paragraphs from "The Daily Worker" which he considered Lena and Brian should listen to. Lena giggled while he was reading, a response that goaded him into further lengthy political exhortations.

Lena was my idea of a sex symbol, a glamorous mum with shining black hair, long legs and a film-star smile who cuddled Brian on the sofa. The two of them formed an alliance against Bill who sometimes stomped out into the garden and revved up his motorbike with a noise as angry as his comments over the newspaper. I envied Brian. I couldn't imagine having a mother like Lena.

In the Hartels' front room there was a cream-coloured plaster bust of a bearded man with flowing hair.

"Who's that?" I asked.

"That's Brahms," Brian informed me, "he was a famous musician."

At the base of the bust was a thin strip of Elastoplast which I peeled away. Underneath another name was incised in the plaster: Karl Marx.

"Who's Karl Marx and why is he covered up?" I asked, intrigued by the concealment.

"He's German, "Brian explained. "Dad covered him up because he's German."

13 Ancestral Voices

The rich have their portraits and family trees. The less rich are lucky if they have a few names in a family bible. We had no family bible and everyone before my grandparents had vanished into oblivion. Even my grandparents were shadowy figures, although one set was still alive.

We visited both sides, the Daniels in their grave in Bow, the Turners at their small house in Ipswich. The Daniels lived in the East End where they had arrived via Harlesden in north London from Devon, it was said, about 1900. My father's birth certificate records that he was born in Harlesden, a respectable Victorian suburb but why Harlesden nobody knew, least of all my father. The Turners were rural, living first in Kelvedon, an Essex village, then later in Ipswich in Suffolk. There were rumours that the Daniels came from Appledore in North Devon but these were never substantiated. The Turners, like many English families, were definitely of Irish ancestry although whether John Turner, my mother's grandfather, came from the south or the north, whether he was Catholic or Protestant is not recorded. Presumably he was not Roman Catholic or we should have heard, although given the archival enthusiasm of the record keepers, it might have escaped their attention.

A few fragments remained. My mother's Irish grandfather John Turner was a retired sea captain who was apparently walking from London to Southend in the days before the railway was built. Whether he was walking to get anywhere or for the good of his health is not known. Perhaps he was walking towards the coast to reach his boat. The story was that he stopped for the night at The Angel pub in Kelvedon and bought it. Being a sea captain, he naturally carried a parrot with him which was installed on a perch in the bar and managed to outlive everyone else in the story. On one occasion the parrot is said to have seized a customer's nose and wrung it until the blood gushed out. The only other fact passed down about John Turner was that he decided one day to cut off his long red Irish beard, caught pneumonia and died.

The pub was then run by his wife, Violet Turner, after whom my mother was named. Violet Turner had six children, five girls and one son, my grandfather, James Turner. John Turner's widow was obviously a capable woman who turned the pub into a successful business but when she died leaving the hotel to her only son, James refused to have anything to do with it. "I don't want anything to do with business," he is supposed to have said.

However, it was in The Angel in Kelvedon that my mother's mother, eighteen-year-old Jenny Morgan, stopping one day on her way from London, met the handsome but unambitious young James behind the bar and became engaged to him.

"If Dad had kept the pub we'd have been rich," my mother often complained. "Grandad has let go the family fortune because of his irresponsibility." This was Mum's version and it seemed essentially accurate. My mother's analysis was that her father had been spoiled all his life by his five sisters and his mother and had never lifted a hand to do anything. He even had a special cricket bat made for him because he was left-handed. "He couldn't change a light-bulb," my mother would say. "Every Friday night he'd hand his wage-packet to his wife, who took all the money except for one-and-six. 'There, Jim, that's for your haircut, the only thing I can't do for you,' she'd say."

James Turner was a ladies man, handsome, well-dressed but not it is evident, very practical. He couldn't even find a house for himself. Everything was done by Jenny's brother, Uncle Jim, a successful auctioneer and estate agent and the dynamic tycoon of the family. He found Grandad a job as a clerk with Shell Oil on the basis of Grandad's fine handwriting - his sole accomplishment apart from his fine bass voice and his left-handed cricket bat. The five sisters married local farmers and

Indian army officers and left Kelveden or went overseas. Uncle Jim bought a house in Ipswich, filled it with furniture and pictures and installed Grandad and Grandma in it.

Grandma's father had been much more successful than her husband. As one of the founders of the Religious Tract Society, he published translations of the Bible and sent them to remote outposts of the Empire. It was a profitable business in Victorian times and with the profits he bought a large, pillared house in Brixton, owned a pony and trap and sent Jenny to school until she was sixteen. Grandma came down in the world when she married Grandad without The Angel pub, and spent much of her energy trying to get back up again.

"She'd only talk to the doctor and the vicar," my mother admitted. "Nobody else was good enough for her."

My father was more caustic. "They spent all their lives social climbing and got nowhere," he said of his in-laws.

Grandma and Grandad had been literally blown out of their home in Ipswich during the bombing. The Victorian mahogany sideboard was hurled through the air to the bottom of the garden. I found it difficult to imagine such a violent catastrophe in the small, dark dining-room in which they lived. There was a heavy, green velvet cover on the dining-table and a large, black wooden clock with brass numerals and a long pendulum hanging on the wall in one corner, ticking monotonously in the muffled atmosphere.

Every morning after breakfast, Grandad shaved with a cut-throat razor that he stropped on a leather strap hanging by the window. He sat at the green velvet table in front of a shaving-mirror, soaping his face with a large brush then drawing the steel blade down his cheek, stretching the skin with his fingers. Every afternoon Grandma Turner slept with her grey stockinged feet on a footstool.

I examined my face in the shaving mirror, small on one side, enormous on the other. Grandad was good-looking with pink cheeks, bright blue eyes and a white moustache. He wore rounded collars and chucked shop-girls under the chin when we were out shopping, a practice my mother disapproved of. She respected her mother as the real source of energy in the house.

Grandma made brawns and parsnip wine and cured hams and organised jumble sales at the church and turned the front parlour into a committee room for the Conservatives at election time.

It was a small, dark house. The coal was kept in a cupboard at the end of a corridor and the vegetables in the bath. But there were pictures.

Above the beds were embroidered biblical texts and a picture entitled "Pale Hands Beside the Shalimar" with an Indian maiden beside a river and a turbaned Indian prince kneeling above her. Downstairs there was a large sepia photograph of a ringlet-haired girl washing a dog in a tin bath with "Tomorrow Will Be Sunday" written underneath and above the sideboard that had been blown to the bottom of the garden, was a large drawing of two pale horses looking over a fence.

But the painting which hypnotised me most was in a gold frame which, Grandad informed me, was called, "Nelson's First Encounter with the French." I looked at it for hours in the dark room while Grandma was having her afternoon nap and nothing was moving except for the pendulum under the black-faced clock ticking in the corner.

Nelson, a young boy of about fifteen stood in a classroom holding his books in front of a silver-haired, silver-moustached master in a white frock-coat with leggings buttoned up the side. To his right was a wicker waste-paper basket with every strand vividly painted. Nelson had wavy, tousled hair and an expression of confidant superiority over the French teacher who was sitting down. Behind, in the middle distance, some schoolboys were fighting on the school benches while a ray of sunlight shone diagonally through the long windows on the left illuminating the scene. Nelson was clearly going to grow up and defeat the French. It was a painting of heroic disdain and adolescent ambition. I was transfixed and studied every detail. Years later I discovered that the painting was actually entitled "Wellington's First Encounter with the French." Grandad had managed to get the title wrong but it didn't make much difference to me. They both fought the French.

The Daniel grandparents died before I was born but in a way

they were more vivid than the Turners perhaps because they were involved with the First World War. They were buried in Bow cemetery where every year we attempted to find them among a large number of angels, caged tombs, obelisks and urns. The November fog swirled around, hiding the tops of the tombs and giving the whole place a gloomy, desolate air, not to my mother's liking.

"They lived in crowds and they died in crowds," she said walking backwards and forwards, banging her gloved hands. For some reason it was always difficult to locate the plot, a symbolic hunt for our family history as entangling as the briars and bushes that had overgrown it. But at last we found it and my father unwrapped the paintbrushes, newspapers, sandpaper, rags and tin of corporation green paint he had brought with him, cleaned up his parents' grave and repainted it. Then he placed fresh flowers in the pot next to the stone headstone with two lines of poetry cut into it.

Ships That Pass in the Night
And Speak Each Other in Passing.

Underneath was written *Longfellow*. I thought it was very moving.

"We found it in Mum's diary," Dad explained.

George and Lucy had obviously loved one another in spite of George's erratic career, which followed his return from the war. There were two photographs in the family album, one taken on Armistice Day showing the family outside the railings of their house with a line of triangular flags fluttering above, the other a studio photograph with George in his artillery bombardier's uniform, protectively sheltering his delicate-faced wife, Lucy, who is holding Dorothy the new baby, while the two boys, Len and Norman in sailor suits, stand on either side.

The war was the great event of his life. In addition to the two photographs there was his mahogany writing-cabinet containing medals with blue and gold ribbons, a roll of Italian lire and the red notebook bound with black elastic of the sort I used to hold my socks up. Inside the notebook was the diary of George's war.

Laconic, consisting chiefly of dates with the occasional exclamation in brackets, it gave the impression of someone endlessly moving around on the battlefields of the Somme and the Italian front:

left Folkestone 5pm
6.9.17
arrived Boulogne 8pm
6.9.17
St Martins Camp Boulogne midnight
6.9.17
left Boulogne 3pm arrived Etaples 7pm
11.9.17
left St Etats 4am
13.9.17
arrived Poperinghe Belgium midnight
13.9.17
transferred to 237 Battery as reinforcements
in firing line Ypres front
14.9.17
4 casualties. First time in action.
Big push commenced 5.30 am
20.9.17
Ypres Menin Tower Hamlets Ridge
Sunday
all day and night
and Monday
29/30.9.17
heavy bombard. by enemy
4 of us on gun trail
3 knocked out
left me unscratched
4.5 shell
3.4.5/ 10/17

The nights of shelling and bridges blown up are recorded as simple facts in George's neat, pencilled copperplate hand. He was an educated but not a literary man, uninterested in describing his feelings, a pawn in the trenches, shuttled from training camp to the front, then back to Blighty with a shell-wound, then back again to Belgium and finally to Italy and the Piave river. He was keeping track of himself. The record of troop movements, casualties and bombs is interspersed with drawings of artillery-angles and very occasionally enlivened with a

comment on the beauties of the mountains or the colours of a sunset.

There was too a thick scrapbook crammed with sepia and black-and-white picture-postcards he sent back to his children from the Italian front. The wonders of Florence and Venice and Bologna were one of the compensations for a man who could never otherwise have afforded to travel outside England. And on the back of the cards in his sloping hand, were the affectionate messages to his family in Bow with occasional scratchings out in the censor's indelible blue pencil where he had mentioned a battle or a troop movement.

George was apparently a loving and generous man - "He would give away his last ha'penny" - but not a successful one. After a war which clearly disrupted him, he worked in Spitalfields fruit-market, then at the Board of Trade, then as a private detective keeping a crate of Guinness under the bed "in case he was called out in the middle of the night".

"You children get proper jobs," his wife Lucy instructed her three children. And so they did.

When we had tidied up the grave and put fresh flowers in the metal vase with holes in the top, we went to Aunt Nell's and Uncle Jack's in the Peabody buildings. Uncle Jack was Lucy's brother, a Spurgeon, a docker who rose at four o'clock every morning. He sent me a postal order for half-a-crown every birthday. We were served tea with sweetened condensed milk poured from a small can but didn't stay long. For my mother it was a trip to the underworld.

The family had come down on both sides, for a grandmother Spurgeon was said to have owned the Queen's Hotel in Lincoln, although we never visited it. The stories of lost hotels were as phantasmagoric as the Flying Dutchman, haunting the ancestral imagination.

"What do you want to know that for?" was a frequent response to my historical enquiries. The past had passed. And the objects have all disappeared as completely as the actors. "Wellington's First Encounter with the French" has vanished as totally as the green velvet tablecloth, the ticking black clock and the horses above the sideboard that was swept to the bottom of the garden by the bomb-blast.

In the future the volume of written and visual evidence records should provide us with infinitely more material from which to reconstruct our histories. But too much evidence may be as frustrating as too little. An avalanche of material may hide our ancestors almost as completely as none at all and as our records become increasingly electronic we may discover that we have failed to keep track of them in greater detail or have insufficient space in which to store them. If we press a wrong button they could disappear. Saving letters and other documents in a computer may be even less reliable than storing them under the tablecloths in the sideboard-drawer.

14 Good Friday

"It serves us right, going to the pictures on Good Friday," Mum said.

I had been escorted in fear and trembling from "Arsenic and Old Lace", purportedly a comedy but one which left me petrified with terror. It was the moment when Raymond Massey flings aside the curtain and reveals his grotesquely scarred face to the audience.

It wasn't even a film with Ingrid Bergman in it. Dad liked Ingrid Bergman so we normally went to every film she was in. I had some terrifying moments in Hitchcock's "Spellbound" where the spine-chilling music starts up whenever black marks are inscribed on white - the ski-marks in the snow and the black marks made by the tines of a fork on a white tablecloth by Gregory Peck, the bent psychiatrist who is being treated by Ingrid Bergman. In a flashback to childhood a child is pushed over the spikes of black railings. I was paralysed with fear as I now was with Raymond Massey and Peter Lorre.

"We should never have gone to the pictures on a day like this," my mother repeated.

We were walking back from the Odeon along the Kings Road. "Good Friday's the most important day of the church year, a holy day when you're not supposed to go to the pictures," Mum informed us.

Dad didn't defend his choice of Good Friday but I was more concerned to know about the possibility of being murdered by a psychopath like Raymond Massey in Rayners Lane.

"Are there many men like that about?" I asked Dad.

"There are bad men everywhere," my father admitted. "They're sick really."

I thought everyone in "Arsenic and Old Lace" was sick especially the two old ladies who stowed corpses in their window seat.

"How many men like that are there?" I asked.

"Not many."

Not many wasn't good enough for me. It only needed one Raymond Massey in the next street for me to be in mortal danger.

"How many?" I persisted.

"Not one in a thousand," he conceded.

One in a thousand! That was enough to put my life at immediate risk. I could see the psychopathic killer opening my bedroom window, climbing in and hiding behind the curtain, bursting out like Raymond Massey.

"Are there any round here?"

"I shouldn't think so."

Shouldn't think so! The lack of certainty in my father's opinion was no reassurance. There were more than a thousand people in Rayners Lane, probably several thousand, so the chances of a killer prowling around Capthorne Avenue or the back-alley were statistically high. There could be two or three killers out to get me if one in a thousand was an accurate estimate.

"We should never have gone," my mother repeated, "I might have known this would happen."

She didn't say it was God's punishment on us for going to the cinema on Good Friday but that is what she meant.

I had been led out of "Pinocchio" when the whale swallows the heroes, and terrified by the black trees with gnarled, grasping fingers in "The Wizard of Oz" but Raymond Massey was a step beyond fairy-tales. He was part of the real world. There were psychopaths walking the streets and it was only a matter of time before I met one. Nobody, not even my father, knew for sure where the psychopaths were and when they would strike. I couldn't understand how he could be so unconcerned about them.

I was haunted by the fear of being murdered, especially in my bed at night as I was saying my prayers, with no faith they would ward off the killer who was concealed somewhere on the premises. I was not allowed to keep the light on and the downstairs hall light was switched off as Mum descended the stairs, leaving me lying rigid with fear in total darkness awaiting my violent end. Every creak in the woodwork registered the slowly ascending footsteps of the killer. I could see him pausing as the stairs turned towards the top. Some nights I could hear him breathing.

How was I to survive in a world of psychopaths?

I imagined living inside a glass dome surrounded by another dome then another, a triple insulation against the terrifying world. There were creaks everywhere. The darkness was malevolent. I was alone and didn't stand a chance.

I had a terrifying dream, a nightmare. A large man wearing a check coat was swinging around a lamppost. For some reason this was horrific and its realism forced me out of bed and sent me trembling along the landing to my parents' bedroom.

"What's the matter?"

"I was having a bad dream."

"What about?"

"A man swinging round a lamppost."

I wanted to climb into bed with them. I didn't want to return to the fat man who might still be swinging around the lamppost.

"Go back to bed."

"Can I stay here?"

"Don't be silly. Go back to your own bed."

I crept back to my bed, frightened to go to sleep again because the image of the man in the check coat was so vivid.

The fears, engendered by or reflected in the films persisted. "It's only a film," they said but that did nothing to help. Horror films were horrifying. People coming home to empty apartments which I knew were not empty sent me shaking into the foyer. I avoided films with a reputation for suspense, gruesome killings and psychopaths.

Michael and I were taken to the Chamber of Horrors in the basement of Madame Tussauds where we gazed at small wax figures being pulled apart by horses, broken on wheels and roasted on gridirons. These were fascinating and not as scary as the films.

"Let's look there," Michael said, pulling me behind a curtain marked Adults Only where a young woman was hanging in the market square with a giant steel hook through her body and blood dripping out of her mouth and down her sides. The severed heads of the guillotined aristocrats with their eyes rolling down their cheeks and their bloody necks were watching from a nearby shelf.

"They pay £1000 if you stay in here all night by yourself," Michael informed me but I knew I would never be capable of staying alone. There was the real bath in which the Brides of the Bath were murdered.

The torture room in the Tower of London was another source of intrigue and horror. There was a wooden rack for making you confess and for pulling your arms out of their sockets, a black iron thumbscrew for squashing thumbs and a pincer for tearing out your tongue so you could never speak again. Most frightening was a large, body-shaped case, hinged so the two halves could be closed with a series of iron spikes inside that came together when the lid was shut on the victim. I always imagined myself the victim.

But I was fascinated by all this horror as well as scared. Michael and I constructed a small guillotine with a metal razor blade that rattled down and beheaded lead soldiers whose heads had already broken off but which we replaced with plasticine for the purpose of carrying out revolutionary justice.

Strangely enough the war did not supply us with many images of horror. Instead it was presented with gung-ho simplicity. Films like "In Which We Serve", "The Dam Busters" and "Cockleshell Heroes" were masculine epics, worlds away from "Arsenic and Old Lace." The presentation of the war was devoid of the sadism and psychosis that it inevitably encourages. I heard a story of a German pilot stumbling clear of his crashed, flaming aircraft only to be flung back into the flames by Australian soldiers. Significantly perhaps, they were Australians. The British never behaved like that we were assured. German naval commanders machine-gunned survivors of torpedoed ships struggling in the Atlantic, but we always picked them up. Much later I learned from a survivor of Dresden, a woman librarian, that the British and American saturation bombing raids were timed for the seven o'clock rush-hour when crowds of civilians were pouring out of the subways, offices and factories. But the war was presented to us without the horror that Raymond Massey's stitched face awoke in my imagination. The British seemed capable of suppressing the reality of violence more completely in the Second World War than in the First. War became a daring-do of commando-raids and gallant Spitfire pilots racing to their planes, not very different from the stories we devoured each week in the "Hotspur" and "Champion".

Our militarism was more subtle than Hitler's and has survived more completely. While Germans have had to come to terms with their past, we can continue in a chauvinistic fashion as uncomplicated as Henry the Fifth's exhortation to the English on the eve of the Battle of Agincourt. It was, significantly, to the film-version starring Laurence Olivier, made to reinforce patriotism on the eve of D-day, that we went to see at South Harrow Odeon in 1944, the only Shakespeare play my parents ever attended. Henry's passionate rhetoric was given full rein but the other half of the play's argument: the doubts and fears expressed by John Bates and the common soldiers that their severed limbs will unite on Judgement Day to confront the king with the justice of his cause was not emphasised.

It was left to Raymond Massey in a classic English comedy to awaken in me the real horrors of the subconscious which kept me awake at nights and made me terrified of the dark. As a Good Friday message it was perhaps more appropriate than my mother realised.

15 Sticks and Stones

I was embarrassed by my name.

The John wasn't so painful. My father wanted to call me Peter only to discover that a large number of cats in the neighbourhood were called Peter. The chief drawback with John was its blandness. Three out of four of us in the alley were called John. We preferred to use surnames or some corruption of them among ourselves in contrast to the practice in school where teachers addressed us by our first names in a spirit of friendly intimacy. John was acceptable, although meaningless.

I also had a middle name, Turner, my mother's maiden name. The gentry, she informed me, always included the mother's maiden name. I should have preferred another first name like everyone else but the Turner rarely surfaced so I was not unduly disturbed by it.

It was the Daniel that was alarming. In Sunday School a hymn regularly popped up with the opening lines:

"Dare to be a Daniel!
Dare to stand alone!"

At this injunction all heads swung round and stared at me while the music thundered on and I descended into a mist of self-conscious agony. It didn't stop there. Daring to be a Daniel returned as a refrain following each verse, producing a variety of smirks and elbow nudging. I didn't want to stand alone. I didn't want to be a Daniel. I wanted to lose myself in the crowd and merge into anonymity. Instead of the intended effect of the hymn I felt I was being pilloried as a freak. Nobody else suffered like this. Nobody else had a hymn named after him.

The hymn was inspired by the story of Daniel, the Hebrew prophet who confronted Nebuchadnezzar and was consigned to a den of lions. *Daniel in the lions' den* was the usual comment when I was in trouble. I began to dislike my heroic namesake and to dread his unexpected appearance at any religious gathering. I monitored the readings of lessons from the Old Testament with neurotic care and discovered that there was no assigned text from the Book of Daniel in the entire liturgical year. But worse was to come. Daniel-spaniel was a frequent nickname but I managed to ride this out. Sometimes we chanted:

"Sticks and stones can break my bones
But names can never hurt me!"

How wrong we were. What was much more difficult to cope with was the emergence of a gifted gorilla named John Daniel. This animal was quite remarkable with an IQ well above the gorilla norm. He could dress himself, make a cup of tea and on good days operate a typewriter. My classmates discovered the existence of this exceptional beast and lost no time in making enquiries about our relationship. Compared with lions in the bible, a gorilla was a heaven-sent gift for them. I was repeatedly asked if he was a cousin or an uncle and was it on my mother's or my father's side. There was even a postcard picturing my namesake who seems to have started life in Sloane Square where he lived a near-human life with his keepers. Later he was sent to America where he became part of the Ringling and Barnum Circus. Even more incredible was the emergence after his timely death of John Daniel the Second, a French Gabon monkey, nicknamed Sultan whose girl friend Jenny Lind, was a Kevu gorilla. In their heyday, sometime before the war, they were a popular couple in the media, much talked about on both sides of the Atlantic. I had no idea whether John Daniel the Second was still alive and dreaded the appearance of John Daniel the Third, thinking the line of gorillas bearing my name might go on for ever. But fortunately John Daniel the Second died and was taken into the American Museum of Natural History from which he still emerges from time to time, most recently in a long, centre-piece article in "The New Yorker" which an American friend sent me, thoughtfully underlining those passages in red ink he considered most relevant.

Running alongside the lions' den and the gorilla was a more serious comparison that also caused me unease. I was often taken to be Jewish particularly as I grew older and the Daniel nose, a prominent feature in both my father and uncle's physiognomy, begins to assume a more pronounced shape. The culture in which I was living had a legacy of anti-Semitism that was widely accepted. My father has grown up in the East End which was

GORILLA JOHN DANIEL II
ABOUT 5 YEARS OLD.

home to a long-standing population of Jews who emigrated from Russia and Poland in the 1890's and early 1900's, in addition to those who had come from Portugal and Spain two centuries before. But he had little knowledge of their traditions or respect for their way of life. His dislike was largely based on economic grounds: he viewed Jewish employers in small workshops in the East End as paying low wages and exacting long hours. His dislike of what he took to be typical Jewish employment practices extended to the point where he refused to shop at Stones, a chain of electrical shops in northwest London. He had no knowledge of the contribution Jewish people had made to left-wing politics or to European intellectual life in general. My mother's prejudice was very similar. "Never work for a Jew," she said. "They expect everything and they're never satisfied." These views, and worse, were widespread and I was brought up to believe in them as truths, although there were inconsistencies. My mother maintained that the best lady she ever worked for was Jewish - kind, generous and a giver of holidays on a scale unknown among the English gentry. And when my father visited the Daily Express exhibition of photographs taken at the opening of the concentration camps at the end of the war in London, he was profoundly shocked. But their prejudices were not greatly changed by these exceptions. There was a strong legacy of hostility towards Jews even if it did not take the murderous form it did in Nazi Germany or in the Russian pogroms at the end of the nineteenth century or in England during the Middle Ages. Hitler's was only different in that it used the latest technology; his racial theories were a modern successor to the religious intolerance of previous eras.

Whatever we fought the Second World War for it was not primarily against Hitler's treatment of the Jews. There is a photograph of the English football team with Stanley Matthews giving the Nazi salute at the Olympic stadium in Berlin as late as 1938. Until 1991 when the War Crimes Act was passed, ex-Nazi criminals who fled to Britain could live here unmolested. Britain was the safest country in Europe in which ex-Nazis could hide.

In Rayners Lane we did not know but neither did we care what was happening to the Jews in Europe. Hitler was evil; there was no doubt about that, yet the source of his evil, racism, remained uncondemned. It was never brought forward as the chief reason for the conflict or even a secondary one. I heard the sentence, "The best thing Hitler did was to get rid of the Jews" uttered during the war years. I was profoundly upset by being taken for a Jew.

Daniel can be a Jewish name. It can also be Welsh. There was a fashion for biblical surnames at the time of the Crusades as there was for saints' names in Welsh and Cornish villages. If the Daniels have lived in Britain for centuries as they seem to have, they would certainly have been Catholic until, like almost everyone else in England during the reign of Elizabeth 1, they became Church of England.

My mother's prejudice was not confined to Jewish people but extended across a range of other countries and cultures including Roman Catholics. There was the Catholic lady, Mrs Phipps, at the corner of Kings Roads, a peaceful, blameless woman whose runner beans we snitched through gaps in her fence. Catholics were undesirable on a number of grounds – for their religion which allowed them to commit all manner of sins from drunkenness and adultery during the week only to be exonerated on Sunday by the priest in the confession-box; for their too-large families (although the respectable Mrs Phipps had no children) and for their connection with the Irish although Mrs Phipps was also blameless on that account. "They'll pull one another's coat-tails to start a fight," my mother said. The Irish were Catholics and Catholics were for the most part Irish, except for their leader in England, the Duke of Norfolk, whom my mother excused on account of his aristocratic lineage.

The Northern Irish were totally different: Ulster was ours as were India, Australia, Canada, South Africa and the rest of the British Empire in which my mother so fervently believed. Ulster was Protestant and British, almost Church of England.

My mother was suspicious of Catholics but even more prejudiced against Baptists, Methodist, Congregationalists, Presbyterians and other dissenting sects, whom she lumped together as Low Church and whose members she characterised as dowdy, unfashionable women, who didn't believe in wearing make-up and whose religious services were incomprehensible because you never knew when to stand up or sit down. The prayers of these strange people, uttered sitting on chairs instead of kneeling were liable to go on indefinitely because there was no reason for them to stop.

My mother's dislike of Low Church services was especially directed at the communion service where she alleged, they would cut up half a loaf of bread instead of using a communion wafer, a barbaric ritual beside which the wars fought over transubstantiation faded into insignificance.

Even lower than Low Church was Chapel, with congregations dowdier and more grotesque, shuffling about in dusty halls on the outskirts of provincial cities. The Welsh were Chapel and my mother's dislike of the Welsh was given additional emphasis by the way they spoke, a prejudice similar to her prejudice against all northern dialects, particularly those of Yorkshire and Lancashire. "Ee by gum," she'd say, "shoot door."

To this list may be added the Americans: vulgar, boastful and the homeland of Mrs Simpson; the French who waved their hands about and messed about with their food, (although Parisian haute couture designers were exempt); the Scots with their dreadful bagpipe music and their history of creating trouble characterised by the House of Stuart, for which my mother had as little attachment as she had for Irish jigs or folk-songs.

The extraordinary thing was that this catalogue of prejudices was universal among almost everyone I knew growing up. My father shared the dislike of bagpipes and Americans although he had less to say against Catholics, Irish or Presbyterians and nothing against the House of Stuart, about which he knew nothing.

In his essay on anti-Semitism Sartre argues that the Jewish people in the new state of Israel will not be the same as the centuries-old Fagin-like stereotypes of the past but even fair-haired and blue-eyed.

One of the functions of war is to fix stereotypes as an immutable part of nature. Germans were always Nazis, Gestapo-like with their skull's head badges and goose-step parades, inseparable from the straight-arm salute to their Fuhrer. It was impossible to be a German and not to be a Nazi although many had been during Hitler's rise to power.

I felt I was as categorised by my name as every German was by his nationality.

16 The Fez and the Khukuri Knife

Uncle Norman sent me a fez, then a khukuri knife, which I believed for many years was a cookery knife. He had been posted to Calcutta as manager of the British Oxygen Company in India, leaving his wife Phyllis and their three-year-old daughter Sally in an upstairs flat in Pinner.

My mother and I visited them on Wednesday afternoons for tea. Auntie Phyllis made small triangles of Shippams bloater fish paste with cress sticking out the sides because she thought we liked them. But we didn't like bloater-paste and only ate them out of politeness because we thought she liked them. This went on for several years.

The fez was magnificent, encrusted with glass jewels, lined with scarlet silk and decorated with a gold wire tassel. It reminded me of the jewelled treasures depicted in the coloured plate in my "Jungle Book" where Mowgli entered the king's treasure-house guarded by a white cobra. I wore the fez for a performance of the Nativity play at Roxbourne in which I starred as one of the three wise men bearing frankincense to the infant Jesus. The fez was placed on top of my blue robe, which had been made out of a curtain. I always wanted to act but as soon as I appeared on stage I became aware that every eye was focussed on me. This reduced me to confusion and in one performance I knelt on the blue robe, which became entangled with my sandals as I offered Mary and her child my box of frankincense. As I stood up my robe was dragged down, pulling off the fez that bounced on to the floor and rolled in a semi-circle. Everyone in the audience and on stage watched the fez as it circled slowly before dropping off the edge of the stage.

Uncle Norman was the fez of our family, jewel-encrusted with honours. He had won a scholarship to Coopers School in Bow where his father has been before him, although George Daniel was generally considered to have wasted his chances. Norman excelled as a scholar, winning a shelf of leather-bound books stamped with the school's coat-of-arms and a silver cup for running the mile in record time. He was my model and I was constantly enjoined to "be like your Uncle Norman".

During his time at Coopers Norman had apparently been very snobbish. His mother called him Lord Tom-Noddy and it was said he would cross the street to avoid meeting other members of his family. But snobbish or not, there was insufficient money to keep him at school after he reached the age of sixteen and he joined his father working in Spitalfields fruit market, one of the series of short-term jobs that George took in the years immediately following his departure from the army in 1918.

My father admired his younger brother greatly. Norman gained first class Honours in chemistry and moved into management at British Oxygen, translating scientific articles from German and developing a light anaesthetic "twilight sleep" to assist pregnant mothers when they were in labour. He was regarded as a genius in the family, able to speak any foreign language by simply listening to one on the wireless and the fount of all knowledge. My father went up to London University to hear him give a lecture and came back greatly impressed. "The lecture-room was full of professors listening to Norman and him only twenty-five," he announced proudly.

The two brothers were very different. Norman was fair, Dad dark, Norman taller and quick-tempered; Dad had a craftsman's patience. Norman carved a B on the boot-brushes so that we would know which was black and which was brown and became angry when everyone laughed. Norman was Conservative, Dad always voted Labour.

After I was born the two of them bought a bottle of champagne and put it under the floorboards to be taken up when I was twenty-one but they took it up and drank it when I was one.

"I suppose I ought to get married," Norman announced one day. He had met Phyllis who was also studying chemistry at the John Cass Institute. She gave up her studies. They were married and moved to a flat in Pinner. Then Sally was born, the war came and Norman went to India. He always did everything quickly.

The flat had a sombre air. There was a large coloured print on the wall showing a clump of wintry elm trees and a ploughed field with a few rooks fluttering about in the grey sky. The armchairs were dark brown leather that squeaked when I sat in them. There was a cream, tiled mantelpiece with a bust of Beethoven on one step. One Wednesday afternoon I picked it up to examine it more closely and it dropped on to the tiled fireplace, breaking its curly head off.

"Oh, dear," Auntie Phyllis said quietly, "never mind. We'll glue it back on."

She spoke softly and smoked continuously, balancing her elbow in the palm of her other hand. She seemed a sad person, left in the flat with just the baby for company. The blue smoke rose up and wreathed around her head. "It's so difficult, Len," she said to my father, "I can never get out." The flat was like a prison, upstairs with no garden. Dad offered to take her to the cinema in Harrow but she refused. "It wouldn't be right," she explained.

I found a tall, dark book in the bottom shelf of the bookcase with an embossed cover and thick plates in deep greens, blue and orange. One of them showed a heron with a frog in its beak. I tried to read it but couldn't make sense of the words.

"I don't expect you can," Phyllis said, "I'm not sure I can these days. It's French, La Fontaine's version of Aesop."

She was very gentle and laughed as she spoke.

"I cry when I wash the kitchen floor," she told Dad, "I can't help it. The tears just come."

"Phyllis comes from a good family," Mum informed me. One of her ancestors had been chaplain to Oliver Cromwell and another had invented the Manton gun, which was used at the Battle of Waterloo.

"Phyllis is good class," Mum said, "but I wouldn't want her life, left alone in a flat. That's what you have to put up with if you want these good jobs."

I knew Dad didn't have a good job because he worked with his hands at a bench.

"I wouldn't want to be married to Norman," Mum added, "Phyllis doesn't have much of a life."

The khukuri knife which followed the fez had a steel blade that curved sharply halfway along its length and was incised with a hammered pattern of balls and stripes. The handle was ivory and the heavy leather sheath had two small knives at the top, one for sharpening the main blade, the other for skinning people.

"It's for beheading," I announced to Brian and the two Johns when we met in the alley. "It's what the Gurkhas use against the Japanese in Burma."

The Gurkhas were an important part of our army-knowledge. Trained in the Himalayan mountains, they were driving the

Japanese out of Burma along the Burma Road which runs from Rangoon to China. The Japanese were trying to cut the supplies from India to China and General Slim had made his headquarters with the Gurkhas. They were the elite jungle fighters, creeping through the dense undergrowth of the Burmese forests to behead the cruel Japanese. They could take a head off with one swipe. The Gurkhas were comparable to the Desert Rats and the Paratroopers.

I passed the heavy knife around and we took it in turns to swing it. It had a natural heft so that when it was raised the weight of the blade carried it downward. We were opposite Mr White's fence next door to the Brown's garden. Whitey, as we called him, had two Pekinese dogs that ran up and down his back garden path like footballs covered in fur, yapping continuously.

"Look!" I exclaimed and raising the khukuri knife above my head I brought it down with its full weight on the edge of Whitey's featherboard fence, splitting the plank in two from top to bottom. The two halves fell apart revealing a vista of the garden path with the Pekes tearing towards us, yapping their heads off.

We scuttled away at top speed and tried to pretend we knew nothing about Whitey's split fence. But Whitey went to see my parents and that was the end of my outside expeditions with the khukuri knife. It was hung high on my bedroom wall on a special metal mount and I was given strict instructions never to take it out of the house again.

Uncle Norman stayed in India during most of the war and wrote letters to us about his life in Calcutta. One described how the monkeys that ran all over the city were periodically rounded up and put in furniture vans, which were driven out to the edge of the jungle where the monkeys were released. But they invariably rode back into the centre of Calcutta sitting on the top of the furniture-van. Uncle Norman was full of good stories and when he was with us he laughed loudly as he told them.

We continued to visit Auntie Phyllis in the dark Pinner flat every Wednesday afternoon, eating the bloater and cucumber sandwiches. Towards the end of the war Auntie Phyllis and Sally travelled out to India to join Norman but Phyllis didn't like the heat or the club life in Calcutta. She didn't like the cows lying down in the middle of the road or having to manage the servants because they all had strictly defined jobs and the one who ran the water for the bath wouldn't pull the plug out to empty it. Sally had nightmares.

"Phyllis is too English," Mum explained to me. "She likes Bognor Regis where her aunt lives. I'd go to India, give me half a chance. But", she added, "I wouldn't want to be married to Norman."

17 Yakusu

Auntie Doll had the Call. The Lord spoke to her when she was walking in the Derbyshire hills and told her to go to Africa as a medical missionary for the Baptist Missionary Society and convert the heathen.

After she had been compelled to leave the Capthorne Avenue house to make room for me she needed to find a home. She abandoned her training as a tailor and decided to become a nurse, training as a State Registered Nurse then qualifying in midwifery and children's nursing at Carshalton and Mildmay hospitals. Nursing provided her with a home as well as a small income. It was at Mildmay that I met up with her again when I was four, having my tonsils out.

She was dressed in a green overall with a mask and greeted me as I was being pushed along on a trolley downhill to the operating theatre. I had never been in hospital before and I remember the blackness descending as it had when I had been given gas for my teeth. When I woke up after the operation Auntie Doll was sitting on my bed in her nurse's uniform with its red crossed sash and blue cloak lined with red.

She presented me with a box which had a mirror inside the lid and a tortoiseshell-backed hairbrush and a tortoiseshell comb in the white velvet lining. I was not very skilled at brushing my hair. Perhaps that is why she gave me the brush and comb. There was also a lead soldier, a guardsman with a greatcoat wearing a busby on a white horse, with an arm holding a sword that moved up and down. I considered him superior to the brush-and-comb set.

Auntie Doll continued to send me presents, usually religious books because she was my godmother and responsible for my religious upbringing, a role she conscientiously fulfilled. After her parents died, she had come under the influence of an older woman who was a fervent Baptist so she decided to leave the Church of England and joined the Baptists. My mother was appalled. "What does she want to do that for?" she asked. "It doesn't make sense. There's nothing wrong with the Church of England."

But Auntie Doll was fiercely determined. She left the C of E and had herself baptised in a tiled pool behind the altar at the Baptist memorial Church in Rayners Lane. At the service she walked down the tiled steps behind the altar and the waters closed over her head.

"I wouldn't do that," Mum said, "not if you paid me. It isn't natural."

Auntie Doll took her new religion very seriously. She read the Bible every day and refused to drink alcohol or wear make-up or go to the pictures. My mother attempted to arrange meetings between her and a series of young men she invited over to our house for that purpose. She introduced her to one of Dad's friends called George from the toolroom but Doll wasn't interested. "I can't think what's wrong with her," Mum said. "You'd think she'd be pleased to meet a nice young man and get married."

But Doll wasn't the least bit interested in either nice young men or marriage. "You'd think she'd be different, being born on February 14th, St Valentine's Day," Mum said "It just shows you. Perhaps it's because she's a nurse. They don't get much opportunity to go out," she added vaguely.

Auntie Doll sent me a book of the Twenty-Third Psalm, printed in black and gold on white vellum with a blue twisted cord down the spine and a series of black and white photographs illustrating the text: a white-robed shepherd in the Holy Land with his flock of sheep and underneath one of the pictures, "Thou Preparest a Table before me in the Presence of mine Enemies" with the shepherd at a long table with the sheep clustering around and another: "Thou Anointest my Head with Oil; my Cup Runneth Over", showing the water running over the sides of a bowl the shepherd was holding up. They were beautiful photographs and I spent a long time examining them, the rocks and the sunset. Then she sent me a book of bible stories with large, coloured plates. There was one of the angel in the tomb, sitting on a rock in a long white robe with his forefinger pointing upward saying to the two Marys, "He is not Here. He is Risen." I was fascinated by the picture of the angel in the cave with the light blazing around him.

Uncle Norman was incensed at his sister wanting to become a missionary. "There'll be another grave on the African coast!" he shouted but Doll paid no attention.

We went up to the East London Tabernacle where the Baptist Missionary Society held its services to say goodbye to the missionaries and give them the Lord's blessing. It was a small congregation in a low-roofed room with a platform at one end. Auntie Doll wasn't very good at singing but she stood on the platform and led the singing of "From Greenland's Icy Mountains to Afric's Coral Strand". Then she gave her testimonial explaining how she had been called by God to go to Africa and asking for everyone's prayers. Dad wasn't that enthusiastic about religion or missionaries but he said to her afterwards she must do what she felt to be right, that was the important thing.

So Doll set sail for Africa in the middle of the war and wrote long letters in her minute handwriting describing how she had been escorted by a Royal Navy vessel because of U-boats patrolling the south Atlantic; then how she sailed up the river

Congo to Yakusu, a small village where the Baptists had their mission station. In other letters she described how she had helped build a hospital, making the bricks by hand before they started laying them, how she sewed clothes for the African children who were running about naked, and how she instructed them in the Word of the Lord. The missionaries had to make everything themselves. She sent back a photograph of herself standing in a group of smiling black children. She said she had adopted a black baby and sent back another photograph of herself holding a small black child. She told us the new Christian name of the child and described how she looked after her because she had lost her mother.

"It isn't right," Mum said. "It's not fair on the child." Doll described how one afternoon she came into her bedroom and discovered a large snake coiled up asleep on the bed. Another letter explained how she was forced to move out of her house for three days while a foot-wide column of red soldier ants marched through.

"We were never supposed to live there," Mum insisted, "it isn't natural."

There were quarrels between the Baptists and Albert Schweitzer, who had a hospital at Lambarene along the river. The Baptists were upset with Schweitzer because he encouraged the patients to bring their chickens and goats with them when they came into the hospital because the animals were part of their lives and they continued to look after them. The patients wanted to do the same at Yakusu but the Baptist missionaries considered the chickens and goats were liable to spread infection and it was unhygienic to allow them inside the hospital. Cleanliness was next to Godliness. Another letter described a riot over cans of meat which had a paper wrapper with a trademark of an African's head on the label; the people in Yakusu were convinced it contained canned human flesh.

Auntie Doll sent me exotic presents: a redwood chair with a seat shaped like a spoon that slid through the body of the chair so that it could be removed for transporting on the head through the narrow paths of the jungle. She also sent an ebony boat with six small oarsmen standing up paddling and three black African elephants with large ears. She travelled to Stanleyville and Leopoldville and viewed the Zambezi Falls.

Then after three years she became seriously ill with dysentery and fever and had to be brought back to England leaving her adopted baby girl behind. "I told you so," my mother said, "we're not supposed to live there."

Doll was in great danger and we visited her at the Hospital for Tropical Diseases in London where she stayed for several months. When she came out she couldn't go back to Africa because the dysentery would re-occur so she began nursing at Amersham hospital with Eileen, a nurse she had met who worked in London converting Jews to Christianity. Eileen had a large purple birthmark covering her face. She and Dorothy set up home together and shared everything, buying a bungalow in Amersham and living there together while they worked at the hospital. Doll announced that in future she wished to be known as Dorothy not Doll and we did as she asked, although it seemed very strange to me. She and Eileen ran fellowship and bible-study classes and youth clubs for the Baptist church and cultivated an allotment and grew all their vegetables and raspberries and blackcurrants which they bottled every year. When they weren't bottling or holding fellowship meetings they were knitting and making clothes to send to Africa. They played games every evening, Rook and Scrabble, but never for money. They said grace before every meal, four times a day.

"They're very good people," Mum said, "but it wouldn't do for us all to be the same."

18 Teachers

I was unable to go to school when I was five because there weren't enough teachers. The men had all been called up. A letter was sent to parents asking them to teach their children at home.

My mother had been briefly a pupil-teacher between the ages of fourteen and sixteen, attending Braintree High School twice a week, a career that she happily abandoned for one as an assistant in an ironmonger's shop before entering domestic service as a children's maid in the Rayleigh household.

Short though her pedagogic training had been, she dutifully re-assumed it when requested by the Middlesex Education Authority, although the Authority does not appear to have issued any specific instructions about the syllabus. Tuition in reading was not required and I did not receive any. Perhaps the educational authorities thought it best not to allow parents into this field. My father read me the occasional story on Sunday nights from "The Wonder Book of Aircraft" which Aunt Eliza had presented to him in 1919 according to the inscription on the inside cover, and I was spellbound by one story with an illustration of a pilot astride a sinking aircraft-wing in a swamp, waving desperately to a seaplane flying overhead while he is eyed by a waiting crocodile. Apart from this dramatic narrative I cannot recall either of my parents ever reading to me. There were no children's books in the house until the Rupert Annuals began to arrive in the Christmas pillowcases when I was five. I imagine my parents could see no point in buying children's books for a child who couldn't read. So reading was not a parental concern in our house. It was the school's job to teach reading and as the school was unable to take me I should have to wait. My sole accomplishment in the reading line was to be able to recite the name of every aircraft in the set of fifty cigarette cards pasted into a pre-war album, but this was a feat of recognition rather than literacy. At all events we ignored reading and writing in our domestic academy and launched into arithmetic as the basis of all knowledge.

Every morning I sat down with my mother at the dining-room table with several sheets of paper on which to do sums. Mum showed me how to add, writing the tens under the line and then carrying them into the next column. "Carry ten!" I chanted. Adding became something of an addiction for me. "More! More!" I cried, covering sheets of paper with sums.

We moved on to subtraction, carefully borrowing tens from the next column to finance the units, then paying them back. I found subtraction as fascinating as addition. We progressed to multiplication, an altogether different dimension where noughts were added to the ends of lines and the skills acquired in adding up were redeployed. "More! more!" I shouted again. Multiplication had an intoxication that adding and subtracting could not match. My mother was beginning to find the home classes exhausting. "When will they take him?" she asked rhetorically, "I can't go on like this."

But the doors of Roxbourne remained closed to new entrants and the school apologised for its inability to carry out its educational duties, promising to receive me as soon as it could recruit more teachers. We moved on to long division, an intricate exercise that involved drawing boxes with a curved front like a battleship and pulling down numbers, ending with fractions. Long division marked the end of the academic road for my mother.

"I can't teach him anything else," she announced. "I don't know any more."

We abandoned the intellectual curriculum and started on domestic science, making biscuits according to wartime recipes – gingerbread men without ginger and coffee-kisses that emerged from the oven as hard as walnuts. But there was a limit to a cuisine based on rations and we moved on to knitting and sewing. My mother became increasingly desperate. "When on earth are they going to take him?" she asked as the months passed. She showed me how to knit and I chanted *In, Over, Through, Off* as I knitted a blue and silver scarf on thick wooden needles for my blue-furred teddy bear Cubby. The final skill in our morning class was French knitting on four nails banged into the top of a cotton reel. A long knitted snake emerged through the hole in the reel; this too became an obsessive enterprise stretching the length of the back garden path. I made purses of rolled-up lengths sewn together, but there was a limit to the number of knitted purses required in Rayners Lane even when they were given away.

What else was there to teach or to learn? Long division and French knitting marked the boundaries of knowledge as far as my home-education was concerned. We possessed three books in the house: *The Motherhood Book*, which had black-and-white pictures of a mother feeding a baby with a spoon, *The Gardening Manual* which had black-and-white pictures of lupins and the *Daily Express Dictionary* with so few words on each page that even I could sense its limitations.

There was no library in Rayners Lane or in Harrow. Mum retired from her teaching career and concentrated on her dressmaking. I sat in the cutting-out room counting out buttons from her button drawer with strict instructions not to push them up my nose.

Finally Roxbourne's doors opened. It was a new school built two years before and like many other primary schools dedicated to those principles of liberal education which were established across Europe in the years between the wars. Because of the shortage of teachers there were at least forty children in every class, but the lessons were purposeful. There was freedom and discipline. We sat in rows and learned to read and write and do long division along totally different lines from those my mother had taught me. We chanted our times tables aloud. We did Nature Study and kept a garden outside. Later we read Walter de la Mare's "Up the Airy Mountain" and "Cargoes" by John Masefield and "The Highwayman" by Alfred Noyes and Anna Sewell's novel, "Black Beauty". We wrote essays and painted pictures and grew beans in blotting paper with red ink. We had to put our hands on our heads when we made a noise. We sang "We Plough the Fields and Scatter/ the Good Seed in the Ground" in the mornings and "Now the day is Over/ Night is drawing Nigh/ Shadows of the Evening steal across the Sky" at four o'clock when it was time to go home. We did Country Dancing and pretended to be trees. We sat in the shelters that had been dug under the playing field and sang "A Froggie Would A-Wooing Go" and "While the Moon her Watch is Keeping." When it was wet outside we did Physical Training on oval straw mats in the assembly hall and listened to Miss Jessy while we looked up her knickers.

Miss Jessy was a powerful first lesson in eroticism. Wearing a short pleated dark blue skirt cut well above her knees, with a whistle on a white cord bouncing between her large, white-bloused breasts she was a woman of considerable energy, leaping about and encouraging us to do the same. Under her instruction we twisted our torsos, touched our toes, ran round the hall, played rounders in the playground and then sat in rows while she crouched on the stage and told us stories.

Miss Jessy's stories were spellbinding epics of her youth and journeys. It never occurred to us that she may have made them up or embroidered real-life incidents. We accepted them as absolute truth as she retailed her adventures – sleeping in fields, meeting gypsies, climbing mountains, being lost in the fog, encountering strange men on trains. There was no sound from the forty of us. Miss Jessy's narratives went on and on and we were totally fascinated by them.

But we were also hypnotised by her plump thighs as she crouched at eye-level above us, her dark blue skirt stretched tightly across her legs, her knickers clearly visible. Sometimes she moved and our perspective on her muscular thighs altered as she did so, but it was an absorbing performance as she recounted her adventures. Her body seemed to be part of her story-telling, and this together with her epic sagas made her a powerful experience.

Miss Casseretto was powerful in a different way, a woman with olive complexion and black, shining hair who wore a red beret and had a penchant for bright striped blouses. Miss

Casseretto was artistic; she drew large elaborate pictures on the blackboard that sometimes took days to complete - children running down the street with their scarves and satchels flying in the wind, chalked landscapes of mountains, lakes and red-roofed houses. It never occurred to us to link her with the enemy, with Musso as we termed the Italian leader. And Miss Casseretto clearly saw herself as going further back than current events to the Italian Renaissance when pictures were room-sized and of

sensational import. Miss Casseretto's art-works dominated the room and she dominated us.

It was Miss Casseretto who discovered that I was naturally left-handed and left-footed. Throwing a dart, bowling marbles, kicking a tennis-ball, hurling a paper aeroplane into the sky were all more easily accomplished with my left hand or foot. Miss Casseretto was not a follower of nature but of art. She instructed me to hold the pen in my right hand and write. I did so and never returned to left-handed writing. Outside the classroom however, I maintained my left-handedness with those skills that pre-dated

Miss Casseretto's intervention. I continued to throw darts, bowl marbles and hurl paper aeroplanes with my left hand and to kick a football with my left foot. At the same time I used my right hand to bang a hammer, use a screwdriver and other pen-like activities although I was unable to switch from one side to the other once I had become practised in a skill. Whether this division between the dextrous and the sinister opened a path into schizoid deviance I do not know. Miss Casseretto may have a lot to answer for. She clearly conceived it her pedagogic duty to produce right-handed pupils and, like other Roxbourne wartime teachers she was not one to neglect her duty.

Nor was Miss Smith. It was her misfortune to be a recently-appointed teacher, to be nineteen, to wear blue-crocheted stockings and to attempt to teach a class of over forty children the classical myths of ancient Greece. She sat on the desk in the front row with her arms around her slim blue legs and told us about Ulysses, the Sirens, Circe turning the sailors into swine, one-eyed Polyphemous hurling the rocks, Ulysses escaping from the cave by hanging underneath a sheep and saying "Nobody." I was fascinated by her stories which were as exciting as Miss Jessy's. One afternoon she announced that we were moving on to Geography. "Oh! Geography!" someone in the front row said and the word was picked up like a mantra so we were soon all saying "Geography!" and then chanting it in unison, "Geography! Geography! Geography!" Miss Smith realised she was losing control and began shouting, "Stop that!" But we wouldn't stop and began banging on our desks while continuing to shout "Geography! Geography! Geography!" until she screamed at the top of her voice, *"Stop that! If anyone else says Geography they'll stay behind for half an hour after class and say nothing else!"*

The temptation was too great for me. There was a sudden, abrupt silence as everyone stopped. Then I said *"Geography!"*

For a brief moment I was a hero. But Miss Smith carried out her promise, sitting in front of me after school when everyone else had left, pretending to read a book while I recited "Geography! Geography! Geography!" for half an hour until the word made no sense and my tongue seemed two sizes too big for my mouth and I was stumbling over the syllables.

The pity of it was that I never forgot Miss Smith's stories of Ulysses, Achilles, Ajax, Hector and the wooden horse. Decades later I was still drawing on her tales of Troy and Ulysses' return to Greece which lodged in my memory as securely as "Black Beauty" and "The Highwayman" and Miss Jessy's knickers.

19 In the Gutter

Teachers were marginal influences compared with the gutter and the playground. The gutter ran down Lynton Road where it was interrupted by an island of almond trees in Lulworth Crescent. It continued along Widdecombe crossing Exeter Road, finally turning into Torbay where the school stood, a distance of about half a mile but one which could take hours to traverse.

Sometimes we called for one another on the way to school. I called for Brian; John Brown appeared like Pan out of the bushes at Lulworth Crescent; Martin was more erratic and showed up less regularly.

The gutter was our thoroughfare for marbles, cigarette-cards, spinning tops, flying aeroplanes and conkers. There were non-competitive pursuits that existed outside the gutter such as cat's cradle and twiddling y-shaped sticks in spiders' webs on autumn mornings to hold against the sun, but the gutter was our major arena and marbles our premier game. It was impossible to buy marbles in the shops but there were sufficient in circulation from before the war. We carried our collections in draw-string bags: one-ers, small clouded marbles with a white whorl on the outside, two-ers, slightly larger, three-ers which were bigger and rarer, four-ers that were highly prized and six-ers, whoppers beyond price. There were also ball-bearings that some misguided souls regarded as the most valuable of all, although it was never clear to me why they should.

We usually played longsy shouting *"Lardy!"* for the other person to start. The bowler who hit his opponent's marble collected it. There were a few variations: *"bombsy"* where the marble was dropped vertically and *"tipsy"* where a hit was disallowed if the shouter called immediately. But although the rules were simple, it required considerable skill to play and we spent hours straddling the gutters and sighting the marble. We collected sets of colours and exchanged four-ers for four one-ers; we traded continually, since there was only a finite supply. Our bulging marble bags were precious possessions and looking at our collections and counting them took up as much time as actually playing with them.

Cigarette-cards or fag-cards as we always called them, were equally popular, a major-league gutter road sport. The cards dated from the pre-war years and were no longer obtainable since they were no longer given away with cigarettes. Their commercial function had disappeared and they evoked a more exotic period which we only knew through the images they conveyed from that magical time. There were two types: plain and sticky-backs. The plain-backed were of older vintage dating from the 1920s and generally more highly prized because they were more substantial and more carefully coloured. There were regimental badges from the First World War and early racing cars and film stars of the silent screen. The sticky backs were more flimsy and more recent: there was the Coronation series, featuring archbishops, princes, earls and barons, arrayed in their robes with elaborate orders and stars on their chests; modern Hollywood stars with blonde bobbed curls and pert mouths and the men with slick shining hair; tips on playing professional tennis and a series of modern cricketers. The sticky backs had a tendency to stick together on hot summer days and were liable to tear. The older cards were heavier and cut into the air more efficiently when licked along the leading edge.

As with marbles, the basic game was 'longsy' when one player shouted *"lardy!"* and the other had to start. One player flicked a card into the air, followed by his opponent; the one that travelled farthest won. But fag-cards contained a potential for more dramatic contests than marbles. There was a game where three cards were propped against a wall and the players tried to knock them down by taking turns to flick another card at them. This took time, skill and a vast quantity of flicked cards. A large pile, sometimes over a hundred, could build up on the pavement. The winner was the person who knocked over the last propped-up card and he collected all the cards that lay scattered on the ground. It was a heart-stopping contest since it was possible to lose one's entire collection of cards in a single game. The scramble that followed the winning hit when the victor endeavoured to scrape together his winnings as fast as possible and the loser debated with himself whether it was worthwhile to try and recoup his losses by physical violence, gave fag-cards an edge that marbles lacked. It had all the suspense of a casino, as card after card fluttered on to the pile.

A simpler game was "topsy" where one player flicked a card on to the ground and the next player tried to cover it with one of his cards. Again this could result in a vast number of squandered cards and again there were dramatic contests where whole collections were lost.

Fag-cards produced more aggression than marbles. We collected sets, swapping cards fanned out in our hands. Often a marauding colleague who had lost all his cards, would smack underneath our hand sending a cascade of cards skyward.

The playground took over where the gutter ended. It was the arena for gladiatorial combats, hour-long fights between battling pugilists, slugging it out surrounded by a huge whirlpool of shouting children. A teacher would try to force his way through the twenty deep circle but be unable to reach the centre. When a truly classic match occurred, as it did between Blakey, a squarely built boy with a back like an ox, and Quick, a tall, stringy thug, the crowd reached fever pitch and the fight became epic. The whole school was deserted. No other activity was visible in the large playground except the shouting, revolving crowd with two struggling figures at the vortex, shirts ripped open, blood streaming from their noses.

Such combats were unforgettable but rare. More normally we played peacefully. In summer the boys sat around in small groups of four on the perimeter of the playground playing fivestones. This was an elaborate game, requiring considerable skill where we took turns to throw up the five square cubes and catch them on the back of the hand. Those caught were set aside and the remainder picked up, first singly, then two or three at a time. The sequence had to be worked through: two thrown in the air while one was picked up, then three, four and five. There were further variations: lamp-post where four stones were piled on top of each other and picked off one by one, while one fivestone was thrown in the air. There was horse-in-the-stable where stones were knocked through outstretched fingers. A failure at any step in the sequence meant the next player took over. My father made me a set of five aluminium cubes with my initials stamped on the side of each one, which was useful when they were stolen, as they frequently were. We played for hours, sitting crossed-legged in the dust.

The playground was the most important space in the school, bounded on one side by heaps of coke for the boilers and at the far end by the brick walls of the lavatories against which the girls hung upside down like fruit-bats, their skirts tucked into their blue knickers.

The girls were a race, almost a species apart. Every morning we passed them as they bounced tennis balls against the wall juggling three or four in the air, calling out rhymes. Sometimes they skipped singly, twisting the rope into patterns and criss-crossing their ankles. Or they skipped in groups with a long rope while two or three of them jumped backwards and forwards chanting "I like coffee, I like tea/I like you, you like me." Or they played hopscotch, chalking numbered squares on the ground, throwing a pebble and hopping on one leg with their skirts tucked in to pick it up. We never played with them and had only a vague idea of what they were doing. The only game played by both boys and girls although not together, was cats-cradle but here the girls were more skilful at transferring patterns of string off one another's fingers. I got as far as fish-in-the dish but it was elementary compared with the elaborate string-designs that the girls transferred from one another's fingers. Cat's-cradle was not regarded as a proper boy's game.

Bash-ups on the other hand was completely the masculine recreation par excellence. In terms of violence and disruption it was second only to the playground fights. Two boys with arms crossed behind them charged around the playground knocking over any smaller bodies in their path. Those knocked over lined up behind the leaders creating a formidable multi-paired machine like a stretched Roman chariot that swept across the playground, around the edges and down the centre, sweeping all other activities out of its way. The exhilaration of bash-ups lay in its communal strength so that by the end virtually every boy in the playground was a member of its collective power.

In autumn we played conkers. There were few horse chestnut trees in Rayners Lane so conkers assumed a rarity value equal to fag-cards or marbles. Conkers took the form of personal tournaments. To produce warriors of steel-hardness they were soaked in vinegar overnight and then roasted in the oven. The rules allowed the victor to collect the lives of the defeated conker so if a fiver smashed a tenner it became a fifteener. John Brown was good at conkers as he was at all sports; he stretched the drawstring tight over his thumb and released his conker with deadly accuracy, smashing his opponent which was dangling passively in the air like a hanging man, into yellow pieces. Conker collections were carried in long strings. It was a short but vivid season which the girls ignored.

The boys seemed more subject to fashions and crazes, switching rapidly from one obsession to the next, trading Dinky toys for weeks then abruptly fighting each other piggy-back for several days before becoming obsessed with paper-aeroplanes or tops. Girls were more consistent, playing their skipping and ball games year round.

In winter we created playground slides, sliding the fifty or sixty feet of their length, trying to stand upright. It was a fearful and sometimes dangerous activity. Often one boy would crash into another and there would be a pile-up of bodies sliding collectively along.

Occasionally during air-raids we failed to reach the school at all. Our instructions were to turn back home if the sirens sounded the Alert and we were less than halfway to school. We obediently turned back as we heard the siren wail. Then the All Clear sounded its melodious note and we turned back again only for the Alert to start up a second time, causing us to turn round again.

We didn't mind this yo-yo journey backwards and forwards. Neither school nor home were particularly attractive compared with the exhilaration of the journey between the two.

20 British Bulldog

The four of us joined the cubs in a pack, an appropriate grouping for an organisation which modelled itself on a combination of Rudyard Kipling's "The Jungle Book" and Baden Powell's experiences in the Boer War. We joined the Second Rayners Lane pack, which met in a dusty hut behind the Baptist Memorial Church, Imperial Drive. off the road to North Harrow.

"The Jungle Book" was one of my great treasures, a large hardback full of coloured plates describing Mowgli's upbringing with the wolves, his adventures in the jungle at the edge of civilisation and his friendships and feuds with wild animals. There was a coloured plate of Mowgli ramming a flaming branch into the face of Shere Khan, the tiger and another of him flinging a sceptre across the white cobra which guarded the royal jewels. There were wonderful poems at the end of the stories:

Now Chil the Kite brings home the night
That Mang the Bat sets free –
The herds are shut in byre and hut.
For loosed till dawn are we.
This is the hour of pride and power,
Talon and tush and claw.
Oh, hear the call! – Good hunting all
That keep the Jungle Law!

I had no idea what a tush was but there was a glamour in Kipling, a hard, thrilling alienation from human kind that appealed to seven-year-olds who would much prefer to be brought up in a cave by wolves rather than by their parents.

Not that the Kipling glamour completely transferred to the

Second Rayner's Lane Pack. Akela was a plump, middle-aged man with red cheeks and spectacles, about as far from a mother-wolf on the outskirts of an Indian village as it was possible to imagine. Bagheera was closer: an eighteen year old King's Scout with tough, panther-like legs and hair on his knees, plus an impressive array of badges, plumes and silver wolves dangling from his uniform. Between the two of them they controlled the group of noisy cubs that met every week and tied knots, played games, and passed those tests in tracking which Baden Powell considered essential for his scouts in the colonial war fought against South African Dutch farmers at the beginning of the century.

It was a successful recipe: the British Raj in India and British Imperialism in Africa, a combination of patriotism, trek carts across the veldt and rough-and-tumble male physicality which was just what we craved.

If Kipling supplied the mythology, Baden Powell provided the uniforms, every item of which became talismanic. Our mothers knitted us bottle-green jerseys on which they sewed wolf's head badges and small triangles denoting which Six we belonged to. Our 2nd Rayners Lane scarves of red and grey, expertly rolled and secured by an elaborately plaited woggle of leather were evidence of our skill. We wore green caps with gold braid decorated with a wolf's head, and one or two silver stars on either side depending on our success in passing an array of knot-tying and other tests. We secured our trousers with snake-belts from which hung a sheath-knife in its leather sheath. We carried staves of ash five feet long for probing swamps, thrashing through undergrowth, killing snakes and tripping each other up. We wore green tabs affixed to elastic to hold our socks up. Our uniforms transformed us.

Every week we bobbed on our haunches in a circle around Akela, shouting that we will *dob, dob, dob* in reply to his *dyb, dyb, dyb,* acronyms that declared we would do our best in answer to his command that we do so.

We were deliriously happy. The 2nd Rayners Lane patch of dusty ground was an arena which neither school nor home could supply. We could be wild. Our favourite game was British

Bulldog, a special treat overseen by Bagheera, who started the game by standing in the middle of the dry mud patch while we raced across it from one side to the other. Bagheera would snatch up a racing cub, throw him into the air, and shout, "*British Bulldog!*" The cub joined Bagheera in the middle and the two of them pounced on another boy as he raced across, hurled him skywards and shouted *"British Bulldog!"* again. It was not a complicated game. Its fascination lay in its physicality, the triumphant cry of capture and, for those left in the middle, the thrill of evading the hunters. It had all the ingredients of a classical circus. At the end everyone was in the centre of the arena except one boy, a bullet-headed, torn-jersied, flailing-arms cub who was compelled to run against hopeless odds into the arms of his captors, to be hurled up into the air to a universal shout of *"British Bulldog!"* Baden Powell and Kipling would have been proud of us.

In addition to "British Bulldog" we strove to gain a variety of triangular-shaped badges, divided into sets of different colours for a range of accomplishments. There were twelve badges from swimming to stamp-collecting, each triangle decorated with a symbol - a frog for swimming, a magnifying glass for stamp-collecting, a watering-can for gardening, a needle and thread for sewing and so on. I set out to collect all twelve, and dutifully polished windows, maintained a garden plot for three months, planted lettuces and radishes, tied tourniquets, swam fully-clothed, picked up a brick from the bottom of the swimming-pool, made my bed for the requisite period and lit the fire in the front room with rolled-up newspapers and one match.

I assumed that we were supposed to gain the complete set of badges if we possibly could. In a culture obsessed by collecting marbles, shrapnel, radar strips, matchbox-tops and cigarette-cards, the cub badges seem to occupy a natural place. Most cubs had only two or three badges on their left sleeve but this did not unduly disturb me. I collected my badges with enthusiasm and my mother sewed the small triangles on to my sleeve until the wool threatened to come apart under their collective weight. I was not especially proud of my achievement, nor did I feel that my competence in, say, window cleaning was superior to anyone else's. I simply assumed that the game of collecting stamps or marbles had been transferred to cub badges. But Akela had a different perspective on the whole process. Mindful perhaps of the one and two-badged cubs or believing that there were more important activities in life than aggressive competition, he took the opportunity to deliver a mini-sermon to the assembled pack as he awarded me my climactic, twelfth badge. Collecting badges, he said, was not the whole aim of the scout movement, which was primarily concerned with those more enduring moral qualities of brotherhood, co-operation and courage. Badges were all very well, but a good cub could not be judged on badges alone. A good cub was one who conducted himself with discipline and integrity. There was more in a similar vein, which I did not disagree with but which I felt was definitely undermining my achievement in gaining the whole set of badges, a feat unique in the 2nd Rayners Lane pack. His comments were, I could tell, meeting with agreement among the rest of the cubs, especially the one-badgers who were grinning and nodding their heads like turtles although, in my opinion, not notable for the moral qualities Akela was listing. I felt I was being put down publicly, even humiliated among my peers. I wished I hadn't bothered to get so many badges, and as Akela pursued his theme, I began to wish I hadn't got any badges at all. What had been planned as a triumph was turning into a disaster. I wanted to rip all the badges off my sleeve, but it was too late. They were the mark of someone who had pursued the narrow path of selfish aggrandisement. I felt I was a pariah in the pack with my armful of badges. But I was stuck with them.

Shortly after this, I descended into delinquency in a way that demonstrated the superiority of the moral qualities Akela had emphasised in his peroration. The four of us were returning from a cub outing brandishing our staves in an abandoned manner on the 114 bus as it ran along the Kings Road. We were clearly not behaving as the responsible passengers we should have been, according to the cub code when in public. The bus conductor stopped the bus, and ordered us to leave his bus in the threatening manner that bus conductors invariably assumed when they addressed us. We exited in some haste and I managed to get my stave entangled in a half-open window so that it swung against the branches of the trees that lined Kings Road as the bus started up again. After a short, clattering journey, the bus stopped a second time. The irate conductor jumped off, yanked the stave out of the window and hurled it with evident disgust as far as he could from his bus before jumping on board and vanishing into the distance. I prayed that he would not report the incident to Akela but my prayers were in vain. I was arraigned before the pack on a charge of being a public nuisance, a disgrace to the cubs and those qualities enunciated by Baden Powell which had been emphasised by Akela in his talk the previous week.

I felt deeply ashamed at my disgrace and attempted to regain some of my lost ground by volunteering to read the lesson at the monthly Scouts Parade that took place in the Baptist Memorial Church adjoining our hut. The cub reading was never popular and there was always some difficulty in securing volunteers. But it was not as successful a move as I had hoped, partly because I had forgotten the self-consciousness that descended upon me whenever I had to appear before a public audience. The Baptist church was considerably larger than the Roxbourne assembly hall where I had performed as a Wise Man in the Nativity Play and the audience more intimidating. Hundreds of grown-up scouts with huge knees and wide-brimmed hats adorned with green plumes assembled in a forest of flags on a Sunday morning once a month. There were motherly Guides in their blue uniforms surrounded by dozens of thin-legged Brownies in their brown tunics. The whole assembly was awe-inspiring in its ceremonial grandeur even before they lined up and marched into the church behind the leading scout beating a drum as large as himself mounted on a leopard skin, bugles blowing, flags waving, and last of all, the line of cubs, dwarfed in comparison with the rest of the procession.

Inside the church we were met with a high, cream-walled interior decorated at one end with a round blue window showing uplifted hands and "Underneath Are The Everlasting Arms" and at the other end, the altar with a stone plaque incised with the paragraph from John Bunyan's "Pilgrims Progress" which from repeated re-readings I knew by heart:

Then said he, I am going to my Father's, and though with great difficulty I am got hither, yet now I do not repent me of all the Trouble I have been at to arrive where I am. My Sword I give to him that shall succeed me, in my Pilgrimage, and my Courage and Skill to him that can get it. My Marks and Scars I carry with me, to be a witness for me that I have fought his Battles who now will be my Rewarder. When the day that he must go hence was come, many accompanied him to the Riverside, into which, as he went, he said, Death, where is thy Sting? And, as he went down deeper he said, Grave, where is thy Victory? So he passed over and all the Trumpets sounded for him on the other side.

I felt like Christian at the end of his journey as the hymn faded into a yawning silence, and I realised by a curt nod from the minister that my moment of truth had arrived. I walked across the polished floor to the pulpit, opened the small door at the back and climbed up the stairs to emerge before the congregation with the demeanour of a convicted felon coming out to meet the crowd assembled for a public execution.

The church was full, crowded to the back with hundreds of uplifted faces and watching eyes. I clung to the edge of the pulpit for support while the scene wobbled and swam below me. I found it almost impossible to look up from the large bible opened on the lectern in front of me with its red ribbon and red arrow pointing to the text. I felt that if I looked too closely at the audience I should immediately dissolve inside my skin and turn into a puddle on the floor. I could already feel the sweat trickling down inside my trousers on to my knees. The whole congregation was undulating in front of me like a roller coaster. I announced the book, Isaiah, and the verse, discovering that my voice was beginning to disappear too, making me sound like a small bird squeaking over the edge of a nest.

"He was wounded for our transgressions," I informed the congregation. "He was bruised for our iniquities: the chastisement of our peace was upon him," I croaked. "And with his stripes we are healed. We are like sheep who have gone astray." I stumbled on, clutching the lectern, keeping my head down, concluding with the grateful Amen and shuffling back down the stairs of the pulpit, across the brightness of the polished floor to the relative safety of my chair. It had, I knew, been a disaster. One or two worshippers gave me a disinterested glance but I was convinced everyone in the church was aware of the woeful inadequacy of my performance and had stored up the knowledge in their hearts. My attempt at penance had only increased public scrutiny of my lot. I was not only a failure as a cub but a calamity as a reader. I felt dizzy, unable to hear the minister announce the next hymn or realise that the congregation was standing up to sing. It seemed inconceivable that they were actually going on with the service. I wanted nothing more than to curl up in a cave full of friendly wolves far away from the human world of grown-ups and failure.

21 Sins As Scarlet

I was despatched to Elm Road Sunday School, a Christian Brethren institution halfway between Rayners Lane and North Harrow but definitely towards the bottom of the Low Church league as far as my mother was concerned. I assume that she considered any instruction in the Christian religion was better than none at all.

The Churches of England - St. Paul in South Harrow, and St. Alban in North Harrow - were some distance from Rayners Lane, and held their Sunday schools in the morning rather than in the afternoon. This timetable did not fit in with our domestic ritual, whatever the Victorian practice of attending church on Sunday morning may have been. Dad worked in the garden on Sunday morning; Sunday dinner was followed by his two-hour nap under *The Sunday Express* in the front room; it was this custom that was the crucial factor in determining the nature of my Christian indoctrination.

He required a peaceful, unlighted interior for his snooze, a requirement that reduced my mother to sitting in the dark darning socks until she could no longer see. The heating arrangements - an open fire - meant that she was unable to escape to a lighted room during the winter months. And as the only Sunday school that functioned at the same time as my father slept was the Christian Brethren, this became the natural choice for my religious instruction. My father was undogmatic about the nature of the instruction I received but definitely favoured the afternoon sects.

The Christian Brethren were a friendly, generous group, less awesome than the Baptists further along Imperial Drive where I had had my disastrous experience with the Church Parade lesson. Elm Road Hall where we met was plain and dusty with wooden chairs, bare walls, plain glass and at one end, a raised wooden dais with steps on either side that served as altar, pulpit and lectern. The organisers of the Sunday School were cheerful in their religious enthusiasm. We sang

> Jesus loves me
> This I know
> Because the Bible tells me so,

and other rousing mid-Victorian ballads.

We then separated into small groups where a pleasant young woman in a printed cotton frock read us a story, usually a New Testament parable about the Good Seed or the Lost Sheep and then explained to us what it meant. It was reasonably interesting, not as gripping as Mowgli and Shere Khan but when supplemented by frequent Sunday school teas of jam tarts, lemon-curd sandwiches and Swiss rolls, at the end of which we received a handsome book prize for attendance, it was definitely worth attending. I received R.M. Ballantyne's "Coral Island", a tale of three children wrecked on a tropical island who created a self-sufficient idyllic life before being rescued by missionaries; and "Mr Midshipman Easy" by Captain Marryat. Brian was awarded "Children of the New Forest", also by Captain Marryat, a story of children in the New Forest whose house had been burned by Puritans but who were working to restore the King.

Into this pastoral Eden, however, the serpent intruded on a regular basis. Sin was an obsession with the Christian Brethren in a way that has since passed out of our culture. Sins were impossible to avoid and we committed them all the time. They were the bedrock of the religion and without them there would have been very little to talk about. Sin was linked with Salvation and the two together supplied the dynamic for our weekly meetings. As an evangelical, proselytising mission, an outpost of the faith had been instituted outside Rayners Lane Underground where a preacher harangued the travellers on their sinful ways as they went in and out of the station. Nobody paid much attention to this and I did not associate the fiery speaker standing on a small ladder with the Sunday school that presented me with prizes for attendance.

It was only when he appeared on the wooden dais in Elm Road that I recognised him, and perhaps it was this moment of recognition that made him crook his finger towards me and say "You, young fellow, would you mind coming up to the platform?"

I did mind, but there was no alternative. I went up and stood beside the preacher who explained that our sins were scarlet, and that scarlet was the most difficult colour to paint over, even more difficult than black. He had discovered this when painting his kitchen wall as he attempted unsuccessfully to paint over a scarlet patch left by a previous occupant. With a theatrical flourish he then produced a large reel of red thread from his pocket, and held it aloft. In the manner of a conjurer performing a trick, he bound the thread around my arms which he placed down my sides, shouting, "Break that!"

I raised my arms, snapping the red thread.

"That is one sin," he informed the audience.

"Now," and he twirled the reel round and round my arms some fifteen or twenty times, "break that!"

I tried to raise my arms without success.

"You see!" he shouted to the congregation. "You see how binding sin is. One sin we can escape from, but one sin leads to another. There is no end to sin. How many of you have sinned today?" He paused, while various members of the Sunday school raised their hands.

"We have all sinned today," he shouted. "We cannot avoid it. Sin binds us as we continue in our sinful lives."

He proceeded to pass his reel of thread round and round my body another dozen times.

"Now we are paralysed with sin!" he exclaimed.

"We are like a fly wrapped up, waiting for the spider devil to come and consume us. We are flies in the devil's web, waiting to be dragged into his power."

I felt distinctly uncomfortable, unable to move, and conscious of his loud voice. "And that is our life, full of sin condemned to eternal death in an everlasting hell."

He said more on the same lines. I could feel my fingers starting to go numb.

"Unless," he shouted, "we ask the Lord Jesus Christ for forgiveness, unless our scarlet sins are washed in the Blood of the Lamb. Then we are set free."

He produced a large pair of scissors from his pocket.

"Oh Lord, Jesus Christ, free me from my scarlet sins and give me eternal life."

And he snipped the thread, and pulled my tingling arms up into the air. "Hallelujah! Hallelujah!" he shouted.

I escaped down the steps to rejoin the congregation as they started singing, "Washed in the Blood of the Lamb".

Being saved was the most important aspect of being a Christian Brother. You were either Saved, or you weren't. There was no in between. It was a momentous decision, and there was no one I could discuss it with.

After another preacher two weeks later had harangued us on the choice between eternal damnation, lakes of fire, agonies of guilt and peace and freedom in a sunlit heaven, vouchsafed by the Lord Jesus Christ, I decided to opt for the latter.

But it was not as straightforward as it seemed. I was apprehensive.

"All those who wish to be received by the Lord Jesus Christ, stay behind afterwards," the preacher requested.

I wanted desperately to be Saved, but I dithered, then sidled slowly out of the door, collected my bicycle and pedalled along Imperial Drive with a fearful apprehension that I was pedalling away from Salvation into Hell.

At the bottom of the hill leading to the Underground, I reviewed my decision, stopped, turned my bike around and began pedalling back again to Elm Road, hoping that the preacher would still be there in time to save me and hadn't departed leaving me damned for eternity.

But as I approached the hall again, I had doubts for the second time. Did I really believe? Wasn't I pretending to believe, and God would know I was pretending to believe in him, and know that I was an even more sinful person than the unbeliever?

I hesitated again and decided that I should defer my decision for another week. I turned my bike round yet again, and cycled back, but not with a clear heart or conscience.

"Onward Christian soldiers, marching as to war," we sang in Elm Road while outside Rayners Lane station every other Sunday, the Salvation Army in their blue and red uniforms toot-tooted and tromboned against the devil.

The nature of the choice presented to me by the Christian Brethren produced a degree of emotional trauma but did not affect my belief that we were fighting a just war and that God was on our side. The concept of the just war is a convenient one for Christians since it makes war possible. Christianity is manifestly a religion devoted to peace, where turning the other cheek is a central part of the doctrine, offered as a way of breaking the cycle of violence and retribution. Yet neither the Baptists nor the Christian Brethren nor anyone else responsible for my religious upbringing ever suggested that Jesus might have been a pacifist. The crypt of St. Paul's cathedral that I was taken to visit about this time was like an annexe of the Imperial War Museum, packed with the marble tombs of generals and admirals engraved with eulogies to their military prowess.

But we were lucky. The Second World War probably came closer to being a just war than any other in history.

22 Jane

We followed Jane's adventures in *The Daily Mirror* in John Brown's garden. Jane was the frilly-knickered heroine with Fritz von Pumpernickel, her dachshund, presented to her by a German count when she first made her appearance in the newspaper in the 1930s.

Jane dashed in and out of bedrooms in constant danger of seduction by RAF pilots and wing commanders. She always preserved her virginity and patriotism but managed to shed most of her clothes in the process. Her characteristic movements were at top speed, slamming doors, escaping from villains, running at a rate that guaranteed her skirt lifted to expose her suspendered stockings or her blouse burst a revealing button.

There was no one like Jane in the *Daily Express* or *The Graphic*. John Brown had secured a dozen valuable copies of the *Daily Mirror*, as he later obtained copies of *The News of the World* and "Forever Amber". Jane imprinted herself on our imaginations as she did on the nation's.

There was no one like her in real life, not even Miss Jessy the gym teacher. Miss Jessy was muscular but not feminine. Jane was the essence of femininity, a dizzy glamorous blonde in a froth of lingerie. The war may have given women a new independence in the work place but it also ensured they presented a grim utilitarian image with headscarf, long brown overcoat and in winter, ankle boots trimmed with fake fur and woollen mittens. Even in the summer months women were rarely frivolous. Hats and gloves had largely disappeared; trousers for women were normal for those working in factories but the fashion was spreading to include housewives. There was a liking for military-cut jackets, large square pockets, padded shoulders and box-pleats. Wartime women's fashions were not sexy or provocative.

But there was a compensating universe and Jane was at the centre of it. Legs were sensational and nylon stockings acquired a rarity value that became legendary. Those unable to buy stockings on the black market or persuade American servicemen to supply them, painted their legs golden with a provocative black line at the back for a seam. And the American pin-up was everywhere. Spawned by the Hollywood chorus lines of the 1930's and Busby's Babes in their human kaleidoscopes, the pin-up re-emerged in American Coca-Cola ads, Schweppes posters and as icons under the cockpits of Flying Fortress bombers and Mustang fighters.

Film stars became leggier and sexier with an erotic impact that was greater than ever before, reaching down to us in the back alley at Rayners Lane. Betty Grable and Jane Russell exemplified the new style, extravagantly inviting, with wide curving lips and split skirts revealing their thighs. My mother particularly disliked their lips. "Such great big mouths," she complained comparing them with the rosebud lips of the film stars of the Twenties. "You can't call them beautiful."

Beauty was changing its shape. The long legs of the pinups, together with their projecting breasts, flowing hair and pouting lips heralded a new image, a seismic shift in popular desire. Never before and rarely since have women's bodies been so shaped by graphic design. The drawings of pinups lolling on black satin imprinted our minds with fantasy images of female allure: unreal, distorted but immensely powerful. The pinup was the opposite of the factory worker or service woman, languorous and passive, in tight, revealing blouse or swimsuit. Jane was definitely not an American pinup. She was too lively, too English and she talked too much. Significantly she worked for the secret service, unmasking spies, helping Britain defeat the enemy. But she was related to her American sisters and an important icon of the war. It was at Boscombe of all places that I met up with the real life Jane.

We continued to take a week's holiday every year of the war, at Charmouth, Lyme Regis, Boscombe and Weston-super-mare, showing our passes to the sentries with fixed bayonets who stood by a gap in the barbed wire facing the sea. Taking a week's holiday became an all-important ritual during the war years, a way of escaping the dreariness of what had become known as the Home Front. Only one year did we patriotically forgo the annual holiday, encouraged by the government's Holidays at Home propaganda, but this was a dismal failure and we did not try it a second time. Before the war my father had not been paid for his week's holiday but now he was paid, even though he was not working - a revolutionary change. The holiday was a great event. We queued for several hours at Victoria station for the steam-train which started and stopped all the way to the south coast. On our arrival at Boscombe, we were greeted by banners advertising Jane at the local theatre.

"We must see that," my father decided. He loved the theatre with a strong preference for the music hall, usually involving a series of vaudeville acts including a conjurer, a juggler, a stand-up comedian and a singer. In the war it was difficult to find music halls around London. The Windmill theatre near Leicester Square stayed open with the boast "We Never Closed" written on a board outside, popularly transcribed as "We Wear No Clothes". We visited Chiswick Empire but there was a distinct feeling that it was the end of an era. The seaside seemed to be the last outpost for Variety, and Jane was here to give it the necessary contemporary relevance.

Mum wasn't enthusiastic, but we went. The preliminary acts included a conjurer who suspended a silver-spangled woman in mid-air by pulling away the table on which she was lying and then (a never-to-be-forgotten gesture) passing a hoop outside her body to show there were no supporting wires and casually throwing it to us in the audience to examine.

For me, this trick was much more memorable than Jane, but I could sense the hushed anticipation in the air as the conjuror withdrew and there was a pause before the red velvet curtains slowly drew apart to reveal Jane naked except for a tin helmet, standing on a pile of bomb rubble. Behind her was a painted panorama of the Blitz. The audience stared for a few minutes until the curtains closed, then slid open again to reveal Jane standing motionless on a rock, naked except for a sailor's hat, looking out to sea through a telescope while a naval signal fluttered overhead. The audience watched in hushed silence until the curtains closed. I tried to pretend it was normal but I avoided meeting my mother's eye. The next tableau was of the North African desert with Jane naked on a tank. Behind her were palm trees and pyramids. The curtains closed and opened to reveal Jane on the wing of a Spitfire gazing into the clouds, wearing nothing but a pilot's helmet. This was followed by Jane in a munitions factory, holding a spanner in her hand. The final tableau showed a nude Jane clasping her two dachshunds under a giant Union Jack on a saluting base while the music played "It's a Long Way to Tipperary". The curtains closed for the last time to prolonged applause.

"She's not allowed to move," my mother whispered, as we filed out of the theatre. "If she moves, she's prosecuted by the Lord Chamberlain." It was her main observation and she repeated it several times. I imagined that the Lord Chamberlain or his representative was somewhere on the premises.

The spectacle of a naked lady was I realised, a valuable trophy to be taken back to the alley. I had not been especially aroused. Jane's shapely white body shaved of all hair, lacked the vitality of her "Daily Mirror" original. Still, I realised what a coup it was to have seen a naked lady on stage. No one else's father had taken them to such a spectacle, and I treasured it as a unique event to be exploited among my peers. At first they didn't believe me.

"You didn't go with your parents."

Eventually they did believe me and their questions became more specific.

"What was she like – you know - down there?"

I basked in Jane's reflected nudity and did my best to answer their interrogation.

The Cinderella pantomime that we went to see that year at the Harrow Coliseum, was a much more erotic event although it was intended to be wholesome family entertainment. I was acutely conscious of adult sexuality as Prince Dando, the Principal Boy in fishnet stockings, high heels, white cravat and short scarlet jacket strutted across the stage towards the anaemic Cinderella whose foot happened to fit the missing shoe. High heels were clearly much more exciting than Cinderella's crystal slipper. I was sexually aroused, six years before puberty, without knowing any more about such matters than John Brown had told us in the dampness of the Kings Road air-raid shelter. Prince Dando impressed herself on my pre-pubescent sensibility with all the concentrated power of the new pinups. Sex pursued its separate, anarchic path. Love was more reliable. I fell in love with Doreen, fair-haired with a cloverleaf pattern on her sandals and ran after her after school every day to where she lived in Torbay Road, not intending to catch her but as a sign of my devotion that was frustrated only by her garden gate. Running was my main courtship activity. I chased Doreen home whenever I could, making sure that I never caught up with her for then I should have had to say something.

Paddy Russell was my next obsession. I considered her the most beautiful girl in the school, which she may well have been in her gingham skirt, white ankle socks and shining blonde hair. But she was a goddess in transit, cruelly removed by her parents from Roxbourne to North London Collegiate School, an institution that earned my undying hatred for years after.

Sheila Goodman, olive-skinned with black bobbed hair, was my next passion, a magnetic girl who attracted suitors by the score in a way that made me aware of the essential hopelessness of male ardour. I accompanied her home in a protective pack of suitors, jostling for position, knowing we were all equally doomed by her arrival at the garden gate where she dismissed us with a dazzling smile and a wave of her elegant hand.

It was all very confusing but we weren't confused. Fragments of American comics, Jane in the "Daily Mirror", the Principal Boy in Cinderella, pinups and the girls I fell in love with at school, floated in and out of my life. They were heart-stirring or arousing, but the violent catastrophic weather-systems of adolescence were not even clouds on the horizon. Cubs and the stamp-club were more important.

23 Rabbits

We rushed around the playground, shouting, "The Second Front's opened, the Second Front's opened!" The news spread like wildfire. I joined in with the rest, although I had no idea what the Second Front was or why it wasn't the first front, or what was actually happening.

It soon became clear. The wireless bulletins supplied continual commentaries; photographs of beach landings appeared in the papers and news films showing dark flotillas of ships massed off the French coast. The amphibious DUKWs crowded with soldiers charging into the white surf with their rifles above their heads became symbolic of the invasion. There was news of beachheads with strange names like Omaha and Utah; the allies had towed a harbour across the channel called Mulberry.

We knew it was the beginning of the end, although we were more optimistic than we should have been. The allies didn't sweep through the French countryside as easily as we anticipated and there were incessant battles over every town and village. Caen was shelled into ruins and there was little to take when the troops finally entered. But we knew now it was only a matter of time. The word liberation began to acquire a new meaning as pictures of tanks covered with cheering soldiers and flag-waving women appeared. Against a backdrop of shelled villages, there were carnival images of rejoicing, kisses and waving arms.

The Americans were in charge although we played that down. General Eisenhower was viewed as a fatherly, kindly man unlike General "blood and guts" Patton who, it was said, forced his men off their hospital sickbeds into the front line with inhuman brutality. "Ike" as he became affectionately known, was the Supreme Commander of Operation Overlord and although lacking the charisma of Montgomery he presented an amiable, genial face which we trusted. For the first time in the war American and British forces were fused into one as they stormed the Normandy towns and drove through French villages. The alienation we had felt towards Americans began to soften.

For my ninth birthday I was given two rabbits. Dad had told me intriguing stories about the rabbit he had as a pet in Bow when he was a boy. It was called Victor, and he carried it around with him inside his shirt when it wasn't at home in its wooden orange-crate. Victor was a Belgian hare, a large purple-haired animal that was his inseparable companion when he was a boy.

I wanted a pet along similar lines, but instead I was presented with two pedigree, highly-strung butterfly rabbits more suitable for winning prizes at rabbit-shows than as pets. And instead of an orange-crate, my father constructed a large residence designed to keep the rabbits in the style to which they had been accustomed. It was a rabbit-residence over six feet long. At one end were the sleeping-quarters filled with straw, leading via a pair of bat-wing saloon-doors into the main reception space where there were a variety of ladders and shelves and, at the other end, the dining-area where a brass basket held whatever was on the menu that day. To ensure cleanliness my father made two metal tools, one resembling a croupier's rake, the other a scoop which were presented to me with the rabbits.

Unfortunately these animals were as unlike the legendary Victor as it was possible to be. They were highly-strung, twitchy animals whose brown splodges on either side of their white coats resembled a Rorschach test. For a time I was impressed with their thoroughbred status but their frenetic nervous systems, encouraged by the size of the hutch, made it impossible to be on intimate terms with them. They didn't want to be picked up or cuddled. They didn't want to come anywhere near me and our relationship soon cooled into indifference if not hostility. They became aggressive and I discovered they could inflict serious damage to the ends of my fingers with their chisel-shaped front teeth whenever I waggled them through the wire netting. When they weren't trying to bite me, they hurtled away at my approach, crashing through the batwing doors in a frenzied escape.

Faced with such behaviour, our relationship deteriorated rapidly. I forgot to feed them and neglected the cleaning of the hutch. Jack and Fred - the homely names I had optimistically given them – became even more neurotic and spent most of their day dashing through the batwing doors from one end of their residence to the other. They were athletic and scrawny beasts, not the soft cuddly animals I hoped for. There is a wild side to rabbit life: they eat their young; they grow vicious claws and possess a kick like the starting handle on a car. The rabbits and I began to live separate lives. I would hurl a few cabbage leaves into their brass trough on my way to school and clean them out at irregular intervals but there was always a strong stench of urine when I opened their bedroom apartment to throw a handful of fresh sawdust on the floor.

Winter arrived, a particularly cold one that produced patterns on the inside of the windowpanes and a urine-smooth skating rink for Jack and Fred. In such climatic conditions they discovered that their hectic rush through the batwing doors at my approach was difficult to stop and they slid the length of the living-room floor and slammed into the opposite wall like cartoon-rabbits.

"Don't forget to feed the rabbits," was now the parental cry every day. The crisis came one Saturday evening, when I entered the house to be met with the announcement that the rabbits had not been fed. Relations had reached such a low that my indifference to the rabbits' fate was now obvious to my parents, who had taken the rabbits' side. I was informed that I would not be fed until the rabbits were.

"I've run out of food."

"Then go and find some," my father ordered.

"I'll feed them tomorrow," I replied, although I was aware that finding rabbit food on a Sunday was even more difficult than on a Saturday night. I was led to the kitchen door by my father, who was clearly in no mood to accept my promises. He opened the door and I was ejected into the snowy night.

"Don't come back until you've fed the rabbits!" he informed me, shutting the kitchen door and turning the key in the lock with dramatic finality.

I set off down the garden path. Snow had started to fall in whirling flakes. It was freezing cold and the path was slippery and uneven with ice. I could see the white shapes of Jack and Fred gazing hungrily through the wire of the hutch but I had little sympathy for them. They were the instruments of my oppression. Where would I find cabbage leaves on a night like this? It would serve my parents right if I was found huddled in the Kings Road, a frozen carcass like those soldiers in the snow I had seen in news photographs. Perhaps they would be sorry then for the way they had treated me. I imagined my coffin being carried through the snow by ragged-coated mourners. I walked up the alley looking at the lights in the houses. No one was out on the streets and the Kings Road was white and deserted. No shops were open. At Lakins the black shutters were down and there were no lights to be seen. My parents were more interested in the rabbits' survival than they were in mine.

I walked back along the start of the Kings Road and turned into the alley at the back of the shops. A single strand of barbed wire like a prison camp ran along the top of the feather-board fencing. Inside the Lakin back yard I could spot various sacks and wooden boxes covered with a coating of snow. The flakes were still swirling down, giving the whole scene a lugubrious and dismal air. But something had to be done. I pulled myself onto the top of the fence. The barbed wire was more difficult to negotiate than it seemed but I wriggled underneath scraping my knees on the top of the fence and dropped down into the yard. The sacks of rotten cauliflowers and yellow sprouts were frozen solid but I managed to prise a cabbage head and some icy leaves out with my chilled hands, throw them over the fence and clamber back under the wire again.

Outside my footprints were clearly visible. I would probably be arrested for stealing but I was too cold to care. I ran along the Kings Road, clutching the leaves and the cabbage head. The brittle leaves were still frozen when I flung them into the hutch; Jack and Fred fled to the other end, less than grateful for their sustenance but I had accomplished my mission; whether they ate their frozen food or not was immaterial. I banged on the kitchen door and was readmitted. Soon after the rabbits and the hutch disappeared but I did not regret their absence and hardly noticed that they had gone.

The war took an unexpected reverse. General von Rundstedt counter-attacked in an action that became known as the Battle of the Bulge and General von Manteuffel made a desperate attempt to cut through the American and British troops to reach Brussels and Antwerp. There were sub-zero temperatures across Europe and 80,000 American troops were killed but the Germans were finally defeated and the counterattack repulsed. Day after day there were pictures of blackened tanks in the white snow. General Omar Bradley and Patton were said to be quarrelling with Montgomery but we remained fiercely loyal to Monty who always appeared wearing two cap badges on his beret. There was a story in the newspapers that American regiments were falling ill because they drank milk in Normandy farms straight from the cows; back home they had only drunk pasteurised milk and we took this as an indication that the Americans in spite of their military successes, were really softies incapable of real toughness.

24 Personal Remarks

Divorce was not on the agenda in Rayners Lane. The only person we ever talked about who had been divorced was Mrs Simpson and she had been divorced twice, chiefly because she was American where such goings-on were commonplace. Of course there were film stars who got divorced but their lives were not seen as models and there was Henry V111 who was the inventor of divorce, which he had instituted for the laudable purpose of creating the Church of England, but Henry V111 had not made divorce respectable and as far as Rayners Lane and my mother were concerned, it never would be.

Families were seen as immutable facts of life not to be analysed although there were of course some very odd ones about. But the word relationship was never used in my hearing and the idea that the marriage vows might be subject to the same scrutiny as other concerns was not one that was ever raised. There were things that you talked about and things that you didn't and relationships between husbands and wives, like the English class system or religion were definitely taboo. Families were taken for granted, and that was how they should be taken. Dad kept in close touch with his brother and sister and Mum with her sister. Even though husbands were away for six years, marriage was still inviolate. Jan in Mrs Martin's kitchen and Cobber in Mrs Brown's were temporary disturbances, which would naturally fade away when the war ended. As a result there was even a certain indulgence towards such affairs. The brief encounters and poignant meetings were part of the bittersweet atmosphere of wartime that became one of its dominant characteristics. Chance meetings and sudden departures were not however, the same as the cataclysmic upheavals of divorce. Divorce was the ultimate selfishness and that was how it was usually viewed.

Lily was married to my father's best friend, Ted Winter, and was regarded as somewhat selfish by my mother. " She's a fashion plate," Mum said, not without a touch of envy in her voice. Lily wore expensive linen dresses; she walked elegantly in high-heeled blue and white court shoes and wore broad brimmed floppy straw hats that looked more suitable for pre-war Ascot than wartime Rayners Lane.

"Lily's full of herself," Mum declared when Ted and Lily came over for Sunday dinner. Lily was slim and painted her nails bright red, a fashion that fascinated me as I watched her at dinner. Lily fancied herself as Rita Hayworth whom she resembled.

Ted Winter was Dad's closest friend. They had known each other since their East End days when they were both members of the Balham Cycling Club and Dad won a silver medal for cycling 186 miles in 12 hours. He and Ted had raced at Herne Hill cycle track and toured England together. They had learned dancing, quicksteps and foxtrots and Ted had won "Evening Standard" competitions. They had been best man at each other's weddings. Dad respected Ted immensely as a toolmaker. "One of the best in London," he said. Ted, like most toolmakers, was quietly spoken and slow, considering any subject carefully before he gave an opinion. He sat cross-legged on the lawn and played fivestones with me. Ted and Lily came over on Sundays about four times a year. They arrived at eleven in the morning for coffee, talked until the Sunday dinner was served, then after helping with the washing-up they sat in the garden until tea. It was always high tea with a salad, sponge-cakes, sardine-sandwiches, biscuits and trifle. Then came the evening entertainment. The table was cleared again and set out for playing cards - always Solo. There were clouds of smoke and drinking and the chink of coins in the kitty and laughter.

I liked company. It lasted all day, and next morning there was the lingering smell of tobacco and drink to remind me of the laughter. Ted and Lily were favoured guests. We fetched out the white starched tablecloth and the Bravington cutlery arranged in black velvet in its oak case; my mother dressed up to rival Lily.

But one Sunday Ted came over alone and a tense atmosphere descended on the house. There was whispered talk in which I was not included, with none of the previous laughter. I hung around the edge of the conversation to see what I could discover. A favourite place was sitting at the top of the stairs where I was out of sight but could hear what was being said below. Ted came and went more frequently than before but always without Lily. I tried to understand what was happening but it was like putting together a jigsaw. There were words I didn't understand. Ted spent hours talking with my mother and father and didn't play fivestones anymore. I discovered that Lily was having an affair. That was a new word that didn't mean what I thought it meant. She had been having an affair with a policeman. I found it difficult to imagine Lily with a policeman whom I envisaged in uniform wearing large black boots. John Brown explained that an affair meant people slept together in the same bed but this didn't seem an adequate explanation since I couldn't understand what was wrong with two people sleeping together: I slept with Michael in the same bed. John Brown said if a man and a woman slept together it didn't mean sleeping, it meant they were having an affair. Ted had found a note from the policeman to Lily in an air-raid shelter and that was the topic of endless debate. It was as though a bomb had dropped. I imagined Ted finding the note and unfolding it. Perhaps the policeman and Lily had slept together in the shelter during an air raid. It must have been an Anderson shelter with a dark, corrugated iron roof and seats inside where the note had been found. It wasn't clear to me in spite of all my listening whether Lily had written the note to the policeman or the policeman had written the note to her but it was Ted finding the note that was explosive.

"Poor Ted," Mum kept saying, "he's such a good man."

She always suspected Lily was unreliable, a gadabout, not to be trusted. I imagined the policeman in uniform with his helmet and Lily with her Ascot hat. Why was the note Ted found in the air raid shelter so important that Ted and Dad and Mum talked about it Sunday after Sunday? I learned of further developments.

Ted had discovered she had been meeting the policeman secretly for a long time. She had been telling lies to Ted and the policeman had been telling lies too. I found it shocking that the policeman had been telling lies because I had always been told to trust policemen. Lily had said she was in love with the policeman.

"She wants a good shaking," Mum declared.

"I shall have to get a divorce," Ted announced sadly one week. That was when the word was first mentioned. It was even worse than affair. There were a lot of questions I wanted to ask but I could guess that nobody was going to answer them. Ted was very upset, I could tell that.

One Sunday I asked him why he had grey hair. He didn't have much, just a few wisps over his ears but Dad didn't have any. What made hair go grey?

"It's a wonder I don't have more," Ted said.

"Why does it go grey?"

"Worry, they say."

For some reason I found myself in a question-asking mood. I asked Ted why he had ears that shape.

"We're all different."

"Your ears are bigger than Dad's."

I found it difficult to halt my enquiries. Ted's features seemed suddenly fascinating.

"Why is hair growing out of your nose like that?"

I could tell that my questions were making me unpopular with Dad but that didn't stop me.

"That'll do," he said coldly.

There was a definite chill in the atmosphere although Ted didn't seem offended. It was time for me to go to Sunday School. Dad accompanied me down the path with the key to the shed. He didn't say anything and I was suddenly frightened at how angry he was. He gripped my arm as he opened the door and threw me inside. Crash! His open hand struck the side of my head, sending me reeling against the wall. "Don't you ever let me hear you talk like that again!"

Crash! His hand hit me a second time.

"You don't make personal remarks. Understand?"

"Yes," I blubbered, "I didn't mean to." I wasn't quite sure

what personal remarks were, but I knew now. He raised his hand to hit me again but I put my arms over my head.

"Is that clear?" he shouted.

"Yes," I wailed.

He had lost his temper, and threw the shed key on to the bench, storming out, leaving me shaking as I dragged my bike out of the door. I had never known him so angry.

The phrase "personal remarks" was branded into my consciousness as if with a hot iron. It meant I mustn't comment on people's ears or the hair growing out of their noses or anything to do with their appearance. It was as bad as telling lies, maybe worse. I vowed never to mention anybody's ears or hair ever again.

Ted was divorced and there was a gap in his visits.

Then one Sunday he appeared with Brenda. Brenda was younger, a slim, brown-armed woman who was a good athlete and had won races at the White City stadium. She had curls and a snub nose but I was careful not to remark on these. She sat on the lawn in her cotton dress, and talked excitedly about athletics and was quite different from Lily. She and Ted got married. "Only in a registry office," my mother said. Mum didn't approve of registry office weddings but if you were divorced that is what you had to do. Ted and Brenda came over for Sundays again, staying for Sunday dinner and Ted played fivestones with me again. In the evening there was Solo and smoking although Brenda didn't smoke. The gap was healed and it was as if Lily had never existed.

Then one Sunday Brenda announced she was going to have a baby. Dad and Ted had always done everything the same. Now Ted was going to be a father too. "Brenda's much better for him," Mum said. "He always wanted a family. That other one was no good. She was too selfish to have a baby." She never mentioned Lily by name.

So perhaps divorce was good for Ted after all, but nobody said so.

25 Stanley Gibbons

Stamps were our windows on the world. We collected them with a passion unequalled by matchbox tops, marbles or even cigarette cards. Without intending to, we learned a variety of historical and geographical facts: that Queen Victoria had been not only Queen of Britain but Empress of India. We discovered there was astronomical inflation in Germany in the 1920s, overprinting the stamps with millions of marks. We knew that there were tar lakes in Trinidad and lyrebirds in Australia and that there had been a British Empire exhibition at Wembley in 1924. We realised that Africa contained dozens of countries and that settlers made The Great Trek to the Orange Free State from Cape Town in South Africa and the first aeroplane flight took place at Kitty Hawk in America. As learning aids, stamps were more effective than most of those used at school.

But we were not interested in learning, only in collecting. Gradually we refined our collections from the cornucopia of world stamps to specialising in definite areas. I collected Basutoland stamps with a large crocodile lying in front of a mountain range, emerald, scarlet, purple and blue leading up to the ten shillings in olive-green. John Brown specialised in commemorative stamps from Malta showing the Grand Harbour at Valletta and the Verdala Palace; Brian collected stamps from the Gilbert and Ellis Islands with the king's head accompanied by a frigate bird, canoes, thatched houses and coconut palms. John Martin wobbled about but seemed to concentrate on South-West Africa where there were pictorial stamps of zebras and gnus, elands, the Okuwahaken Falls and a biplane over Windhoek.

We met in each other's houses, except for the Martin house which we were forbidden to enter. There were professional formalities to our meetings, unlike some of our other gatherings. We behaved like middle-aged archivists, spreading our collections over the dining-room table and examining the watermarks by holding our specimens up to the light. The watermark was the secret message of the stamp. We then checked the number of perforations through Brian's large black-handled magnifying glass, and scrutinised the backing to the paper. We debated whether they had been torn from their envelopes or gently soaked. We used paper hinges and brandished our tweezers about theatrically, picking up the stamps with care and sliding them across the table to one another.

The albums were precious trophies; the great divide was between loose-leaf and bound. Brian had the supreme *object d'art*, a glossy black loose-leaf album with tissue-paper between each page. John Brown possessed a scuffed but interestingly bound red cloth album with pictures of rare stamps at the top of each page; I was given a green hardback, loose-leaf album for my birthday; John Martin had a bound crimson album without pictures. We swapped stamps as we swapped marbles and cigarette-cards, with passion and precision. We purchased packs containing five hundred assorted stamps and sifted through them carefully, like panhandlers searching for gold, hoping to discover a penny black or a Mauritius blue that the Harrow stamp shop had overlooked. Some stamps were plain, especially the modernist fascist ones: Hitler's functional face isolated on a plain background lacked the baroque detail we valued and Mussolini too was without fascination. The stamps we treasured were those with elaborately engraved pictures showing rubber-tapping in Ceylon or lace-making in St Helena.

But our interest was essentially more financial than aesthetic or historical. We were hoping to stumble on a fortune and we looked up the value of each stamp in the Stanley Gibbons catalogue and totted them up conscientiously, reckoning their value according to the condition, mint or used and consulting the catalogue with the obsession of investors consulting the index of stocks and shares. Stanley Gibbons was our bible, a thick glossy-paged, encyclopaedic work profusely illustrated with columns of figures under the illustrations. Looking up a Victorian penny red with different letters in the bottom corners was a considerable feat of research; it was easy to confuse an item worth threepence with a similar one worth £300.

This made the Stanley Gibbons a treasure hunt full of drama and excitement. A near miss, a used specimen instead of mint, was greeted with cries of frustration and anguish. We were haunted by the great treasures of the past, especially the mid-nineteenth century Postage Due from New Guinea with its clipped corners, the ship in the centre scarcely visible through a fog of black ink. It was the only one in existence and worth £7000. But there were other near misses - a block of four Mauritius that would have been worth thousands of pounds if only the queen's head had been printed upside down; a cut instead of a perforated edge; a cobalt instead of a dark blue. We were so close to being millionaires it was unbearable.

My father was unenthusiastic in his assessment of stamp collecting. "I've never known a hobby where mistakes were worth more than a job properly done," he said scathingly. I dismissed my father's judgement; he didn't understand the value of rarity or the romance of stamps. We speculated on whether it was possible to obtain a job in the Waterlow printing factory and then hide after the employees had left for the night so we could print a page of inverted heads.

We formed a stamp club including Henry Goldberg, whose father was a postman. Mr Goldberg was generous with stamps and used-covers. One day he might discover a penny-black on an envelope that had slipped down between the pigeonholes in the sorting-office for forty or fifty years. We had heard of such stories. Then we would all be rich beyond our wildest dreams. The King had a fabulous stamp collection, worth millions. It was simply a matter of collecting the right stamps plus a little luck.

The club was a serious undertaking quite different from our random meetings in separate houses. We drew up a list of rules in a hardback exercise book and set a weekly subscription of sixpence, taking it in turns to spend at Harrow stamp shop, buying stamps which we then awarded ourselves as prizes for competitions. The owner of Harrow stamp shop was a rarity in himself, an ancient, bald-headed gentleman with a curving tortoise shell ear-trumpet that it was necessary to yell down.

"Have you any Dahomey triangles?" I'd bellow and he shuffled off to the back of the shop and return with the required stamps elegantly arranged on squared paper. Most of his stamps were far too expensive; we usually settled for a few moderately-priced items plus a bulging pack of bargain assortment that included dozens of German overprints, the French figure of Liberty sowing seed from a basket held against her hip and the boring Edward V111 with his crown set to one side.

Henry Goldberg's house was my favourite meeting place. Everywhere else we were allowed in under sufferance, openly regarded as nuisances and lucky to receive a glass of water and a plain biscuit but Henry Goldberg's mother treated us as proper guests. "Come and sit down," she said. Nobody else ever asked us to sit down. We were offered orange squash, buns with strawberry jam and wartime cream inside and apple cakes with honey. On the wall was a framed certificate with a row of green orange trees full of fruit and underneath square Hebrew letters, the first I had ever seen, explaining that a tree had been planted for Henry in Israel. On the door-frames were small containers of metal that Henry said contained the Ten Commandments written in tiny letters and rolled up so tightly they could fit inside the container. The words must have been so small nobody could read them. I looked at them, intrigued that anyone should bother to do such a thing.

We played games using the Stanley Gibbons as a source book. Which country's stamp had a geyser on it? How much was a mint North Borneo Clouded Leopard worth? Then we awarded prizes and collected subscriptions for the following week. The club lasted for several years but eventually faded as our enthusiasm for stamps waned. We decided to sell up. We carried our valuable collection albums into the stamp-shop where Ear-trumpet had been replaced by a younger man who flicked over the leaves and slowly shook his head.

"I'm afraid I can't offer you more than that," he said, naming a sum so small for each album that we wondered whether we had heard correctly. Our carefully mounted collections, immaculately positioned on loose-leaf pages, which had taken years to assemble – was this all they were worth? "But Stanley Gibbons catalogue says they're worth much more than that," we pointed out, relying on our hero's authority to impress. The man shrugged his shoulders. "We're not Stanley Gibbons," he explained. "Perhaps you should try them."

We realised it was hopeless. Stanley Gibbons was not the gold standard valuation we had believed but only a price-list for a shop in London. We felt we had been duped. "That's all I can offer," the assistant said, turning away. Our idol had feet of clay. We took the notes and a few coins and shared them out amongst us but I experienced a deep sense of betrayal. My collection was worth much more. Stanley Gibbons had led us up the garden path with his catalogue of watermarks, inverted heads and shades of cobalt.

My father was unsurprised when I told him of our transaction.

"I never thought stamp collecting was based on very sound principles," he said. "You've discovered buying's one thing, selling's another," he added more sympathetically.

Stamp-collecting was a passion he had never understood.

26 Friend or Foe?

The Italian prisoners of war wandered freely around Rayners Lane. They were mostly small, dark-haired men in crumpled overalls without insignia or badges who seemed resigned and bored and spent most of their time hanging over the railway bridge opposite the Underground station. Sometimes they gathered in small groups outside the British Restaurant, an asbestos hut smelling of boiled cabbage where my mother took me occasionally when she was fed up with cooking.

We wondered why the Italians didn't try to escape, for escaping was a matter of honour for prisoners in *The Hotspur* and *The Champion*. But the Italians appeared content to stay in Rayners Lane and gradually it dawned on us that Rayners Lane might not be such a bad place to stay compared with Monte Cassino or Pisa where there was intensive fighting as the Americans and British moved up Italy. We debated the problem as we hung over the bridge a few yards away from the prisoners.

"They should escape."

"Where can they go?"

"They can reach the coast, then they can steal a fishing boat and sail to France."

"What good would that do? They'd get killed in France or blown up by a German tank."

"They could sail all the way to Italy."

"Italy's too far."

"I'd escape anyway."

"I wouldn't."

The subjects of our debate looked at us and smiled. Perhaps

they understood what we were talking about. Because their uniforms lacked badges and flashes they seem more like garage-mechanics than soldiers. Compared with the American soldiers and airmen who had appeared like aliens from another planet, the Italians fitted into the wartime atmosphere of Rayners Lane quite naturally. They nodded to us and on one occasion one of them waved his hand and shook his head vigorously as we climbed up on the parapet of the bridge over the railway and walked along it. He was concerned about our safety; perhaps he had children of his own.

Our level of ignorance about the Italians, the Eye-ties as they were sometimes called, meant that we continued to regard them as the enemy even though Italy had declared war on its former ally Germany, in October 1943. We knew nothing about that and nobody discussed it. It remained one of the best-kept secrets of the war as far as we were concerned. The Italians suffered the additional stigma of being regarded as the worst soldiers in the world. The Pathe newsreels of thousands of them shuffling miserably along, ten abreast, with their hands up, holding white flags, only served to reinforce their position at the bottom of the fighting league. In popular estimation the Italians ranked below even the Americans as soldiers. And unlike our respect for German achievements there was no comparable admiration for Italian engineering or Italian art. They were the failures of Europe, incapable of fighting and dominated by Musso, the archetypal, spaghetti-eating, fat Italian.

More significantly I knew nothing about fascism except that it was occasionally used as a synonym for Nazi Germany. I had never heard of the Spanish Civil War and never heard it mentioned. We were fighting the Nazis not fascism and the Italians continued to be the enemy though they were officially on our side. Theoretically at liberty, they shuffled about Rayners Lane in their overalls, looking much like the factory mechanics many of them probably were.

The Americans, our official allies, were regarded with less affection than the Italians. They were seen as strange beings of exceptional size, criticised as boastful and arrogant in their smooth, officer-style uniforms which made them seem remote from our rough-uniformed troops. They were reputed to seduce our girls while the British boyfriends were away fighting, so that sexual treachery was added to their crimes. They imagined they were winning the war with their money, when in reality it was we who were winning it with our courage.

Considering that they were our allies, the criticism of American soldiers revealed a massive failure of government public relations. There were black US soldiers too, the first black people I had ever seen but their blackness was a mystery to us; we had no knowledge of American slavery and none of the apartheid that continued to exist in American forces stationed in Britain. Nor did we realise that the Americans were mainly second-generation European immigrants. We had no awareness of how an American soldier might feel about being sent back to die in a continent his family had striven to escape from. There was no understanding of American history, culture or politics only the repeated charge that the Americans had entered this war late and the First World War even later and that if Churchill's mother hadn't been American they probably wouldn't have entered at all.

But as with all stereotypes there were contradictions. The B 17 Flying Fortress Bombers – the Flying Forts as they were affectionately called – became the most popular bomber-plane of the war as the Spitfire was the most celebrated fighter. Its range and armaments were recognised as unique. Every night at seven o'clock the sky grew dark with planes and our mantelpiece rattled as the squadrons flew overhead on the thousand-bomber saturation raids on Cologne followed by daylight raids on Berlin, Hamburg, Dusseldorf, Dresden and every other major German city. In this holocaust of fire the American Flying Forts with their crews of ten and their tail-gunners were seen as the instruments of a just revenge. There was something about their huge silver bodies that made them seem like avenging angels, unlike the squat black Lancasters and Halifaxes of the RAF, camouflaged for night-raids. The Flying Fortresses were, like the Americans, supremely visible and supremely confident. We identified with them and worshipped their massive firepower as our own.

27 Spitfire

Few toys were manufactured during the war years. This provided the excuse for my father making them. In a previous century he would probably have been a toymaker working in wood but he was born into an industrial age and compelled during the war-years into making fuses for shells and bombs.

After a short period as an office boy in Limehouse Docks in London when he left school at 14, he moved into toolmaking. This was before the days of formal apprenticeship but he was a natural craftsman. My mother had only a hazy idea of what he was doing. "I thought when we first met, he made hammers in a shop," she explained, "because he talked about a shop, and said he made tools." Such a mistake was understandable. In fact the tools fitted into giant presses and stamped out hundreds of thousands of copies. He fashioned the steel from the draftsman's drawings; it was skilled precision-work with tolerances of a thousandth of an inch and toolmakers regarded themselves as the elite of the factory's work force even though they were required to start work in the morning an hour earlier than the typists and compelled to punch a time-clock as they entered and left the building. The time-clock was an object of resentment for my father and many of the other toolmakers who felt insulted by its assumption that they would not be on time. As a result my father was often deliberately later than necessary in the mornings because fifteen minutes pay was automatically deducted after six minutes lateness.

Perhaps it was the same resentment that was responsible for the toolmakers making a variety of "foreigners" as they were called: cigarette lighters, spare parts for cars, or in my father's case, toys. How many thousands of hours were lost to the war effort by the manufacture of toys and cigarette lighters is impossible to estimate but it must have been considerable. Only the presence of bright wood-shavings rather than metal waste in the toolroom made the subversive activity observable, but this does not seem to have deterred my father, whose toys involved a substantial amount of wood-turning.

His first two Christmas presents were Short Sunderland flying boats for Michael and me in 1940. Silver-hulled with maroon floats and underbodies, they were handsome planes even if they failed to stand up on their floats and sank to the wings - an ignominious position for a seaplane in our critical five-year-old eyes. They had perspex front windows, an aerial stretching from cockpit to tail-fin and transfer markings which included our initials and the date.

The following year Father Christmas produced two anti-aircraft guns that could be loaded and fired, emitting a blue cloud of smoke and a whiff of cordite as the shell shot out with sufficient force to topple a lead soldier over. These guns were a great advance on the passive flying-boats. The firing mechanism was activated by a plunger on the breech which released a lever that struck a knurled knob filled with the heads of red matches. The gun barrel could be raised and lowered with a worm-thread and the body was painted in khaki and green camouflage; there were rubber tyres on the large wheels. Our names and the date were inscribed on each breech-block.

Why my father, who disliked war, should have spent so much time making war toys was a question that was never raised. The idea that boys should be brought up to play with weapons was so deeply ingrained it appeared natural. Only Brenda, Ted Winter's new wife, proclaimed that she would never buy her son, Tony, a toy pistol. But she was generally regarded as an eccentric idealist. It was as natural for boys to play at killing as for girls not to.

However, the gender divide exercised my father's skills since he clearly felt he could not make anti-aircraft guns and Short Sunderland flying boats for my cousin Sally. So for the following two years he concentrated on less militaristic presents: a large double-fronted dolls' house with fir trees in tubs at the entrance, hall stairs, wallpapered rooms, and tiny light switches in every room that illuminated the hanging bowls. He then built a sewing machine that was all metal and was manufactured entirely in the factory. In man-hours it must have been the equivalent of several bomb fuses. It operated a running stitch and a chain-stitch and was a working miniature version of its grown-up counterpart.

The following year he returned to war toys inspired by the doll's house and constructed two mediaeval fortresses with prisons, barred windows and studded doors. There was a ratchet-operated drawbridge, underground cellars, and above each entrance arch, a metal shield bearing a dagger dripping three drops of blood *gules* with our initials and date. These came to us via Father Christmas in whom I fervently believed and to whom I wrote a list of requests every year addressed to *Father Christmas, Greenland* which I posted in the letterbox at the corner of Capthorne Avenue. I clung devotedly to my faith even though I knew in another part of my mind that my father was making the forts in the kitchen which was full of smoke in the evenings as he burned the masonry joints of the round tower into the wood with irons heated on the gas ring. It was impossible for me not to know what was going on, but I persisted in my belief not only because the goods arrived on Christmas Day but because it was impossible not to believe. Belief seemed natural and I found no difficulty at all in reconciling my awareness that the forts were being constructed in the kitchen and that Father Christmas existed. There was some talk that Dad sent them to Father Christmas but this was hardly necessary. What was important was the fact that all grown-ups told me that Father Christmas was real. It was inconceivable that there could be a universal conspiracy to deceive me. It would mean all the grownups in Britain getting together and hatching a story, which covered every manifestation of Christmas - every department store, every book and every mention of Santa Claus. So I believed with that trust in the honesty of grown-ups which is instinctive. I believed as I believed in Jesus and in the way babies were born. Christmas brought all three together in one festival.

The final toy was the Spitfire, the *ne plus ultra* of British wartime glamour, the plane that had single-handedly won the Battle of Britain, inseparable from the young men who ran across the grass to take off against the German bombers. It was impossible to be too patriotic or too sentimental about the Spitfire. Small, defiant, agile, it twisted through the sky symbolic of our stand against Goliath. My father set out to reproduce the Spitfire with as faithful an accuracy as he could manage. With typical care, he wrote to the War Office asking for an exact sample of the blue for the underbody and the camouflage markings for the fuselage. The War office replied by despatching an official to our house, clearly suspicious that there might be an underground cell in Capthorne Avenue sending coded messages to Berlin about the colours of the Spitfire four years after the Battle of Britain was over. I listened to muffled discussions in the dining-room. Satisfied that my father was more in touch with Father Christmas than the Luftwaffe, the official departed. My father set about the serious business of designing an undercarriage mechanism that would retract and lock when the wheels were down, in the wing-thickness of half an inch. It was a taxing problem that was finally solved after several hundred more hours of the firm's time. The Spitfires were made and delivered to our pillow cases by Father Christmas in elegant plywood boxes lined with dark blue velvet.

The Spitfire was the last of the war-toys. Forts and guns returned to the shops after the war but Father Christmas never returned. I was finally forced to admit that he might not exist. For me he was a major casualty of the Second World War.

28 Mass Production

Inspired by the praise lavished on his Christmas toys, my father turned his thoughts to toy-making on a grander scale. He would mass-produce toy trains which would sell in their thousands and free him for ever from the drudgery of the factory system. Mass production was the key to wealth and happiness.

"Where will you do that?" Mum asked. She was apprehensive that the house might be taken over as the front room had been taken over by the billiard table.

"In the shed at the bottom of the garden."

"All right then," she agreed reluctantly.

Dad set to work installing two large upright drilling machines and a circular saw on the bench. He ordered a supply of wooden crates, which filled the bottom of the garden and reached up over the alley like the Leaning Tower of Pisa. From these he would fashion the wheels and make the carriages. Each train set would consist of a bright red engine, shaped like the Coronation Scot with a sloping front, pulling three open carriages with a guard's van. He started an account book detailing his materials and expenses.

"Mass-production's the answer," he declared.

I was familiar with the concept of mass-production because it formed one of the ongoing debates in our house in which my parents took opposite sides as they did on practically everything. My mother was a devotee of work done by hand.

"Any work done by hand is superior," she insisted. "That's why ladies want their underclothes made by hand." This was an end to the matter as far as my mother was concerned.

But my father believed equally strongly in the superiority of machine work.

"Stitching by machine is neater and more accurate," he pointed out. "Stitching by hand can never rival that done by machine."

"Don't be silly," Mum replied.

Sewing was one of the few topics about which she was confident she knew more than Dad. "The best clothes are always made by hand. Look at Savile Row tailors. They make all their gentlemen's suits by hand."

"That's because customers are individually fitted," Dad pointed out, "not because the actual stitching is superior."

For my mother this was a ridiculous absurdity.

"Hand-stitching is what customers pay for," she said. "They don't pay for machine-work."

"What they're paying for is the individual attention," Dad insisted, "not the workmanship."

My father's logic carried no weight at all with Mum. "Anyone can buy clothes run up by machine," she answered. "People in Rayners Lane buy all their clothes off the peg." My mother always managed to get considerable disdain into the expressions *run up* and *off the peg*, implying a level of workmanship so low it was not worth consideration. But my father believed in his position with equal sincerity.

"The workmanship at Fords is better than at Rolls Royce," he informed us, "because at Rolls Royce the components can be fitted individually by hand, but at Ford they have to be accurate to a thousandth of an inch. At Rolls Royce the parts can be bodged. With mass-production everything has to be spot-on."

This example also left my mother unmoved.

"Everyone knows that a Rolls Royce is better than a Ford," she responded triumphantly.

As we didn't possess either a Rolls Royce or a Ford, I found this discussion rather theoretical.

The debate had many ramifications and took a variety of forms including the political. "Mass production means more people can have a car if they want one, and not just the rich," Dad said. For Mum this was proof positive that mass-production was inferior.

"I don't envy the rich their money," she replied. "It means they can employ people like us to work for them." She would like to have been driven around in a car instead of waiting at bus-stops, especially a Rolls Royce like the one in which she had been photographed wearing a white fur-collared coat sitting beside the chauffeur in the South of France.

For my father the machine offered hope, specifically the machines he had installed in the shed at the bottom of the garden. The process of tooling-up began, with the manufacture at the factory of special steel chucks for drilling out the wheels. The painting of the train sets, each carriage a different colour, was to be carried out by spray-gun and he devised a series of experiments with different thicknesses of paint: grey undercoats followed by bright pink, blue and yellow gloss finishes, squirting them on to prepared surfaces. Mum's fears of domestic invasion began to be justified. The smell of paint permeated the house. The upstairs rooms were fitted out with drying racks and we experimented with transfers for the front of the engines, leopards and flying eagles.

The additional labour-force required for the move into mass production was recruited from my friends in the alley. John Brown, Brian Hartel, John Martin and I were hired at sixpence an hour rising to ninepence if we worked satisfactorily. We were shown how to operate the tower-drill and given a training session for which we were paid the same hourly rate, since Dad believed in strict trade-union principles. A sales-force was recruited from friends and relatives including Auntie Marjorie, Beryl Brown and Lena Hartel. Auntie Marjorie arrived with a large suitcase into which the completed train-sets were loaded, each one carefully wrapped in tissue-paper ready for the waiting world.

The train-sets were popular and demand outstripped supply. The labour force worked happily for three hours every Saturday afternoon in a shower of golden wood shavings, only marred, as far as I was concerned, by the promotion of my friends to ninepence an hour while I languished at sixpence because, in my father's estimation, I was not such a dedicated worker.

Each locomotive and carriage was sprayed with grey undercoat, sandpapered and then given two topcoats of gloss paint. The wheels were left plain and varnished. The front room was full of red locomotives, ranged in rows like marshalling yards and each bedroom assumed the appearance of a goods yard of small trucks waiting to be connected up. I discovered a certain facility for transferring the eagles and leopards on to the fronts of the engines and was promoted to ninepence an hour. Dad meticulously checked the workmanship of his labour-force, examining the wheels on the axles and handing back anything below standard. We took turns at the drilling machines, lowering the chuck into the wood, watching the curved shape of the wheel emerge from the flurry of shavings. The suitcases were filled again and again.

"Five shillings isn't enough, Len," Auntie Marjorie said,

packing another suitcase full of trains. "It's giving them away. I can get seven and six."

"If you can get more you keep it," Dad replied, "it's your commission."

"Don't be silly, Len, it's yours. You made them," Marjorie insisted.

In this atmosphere of ruthless capitalism we produced trains all summer into the autumn. At every level the project was a resounding success except at the level at which it was intended. We never made enough profit to enable my father to retire from factory-life.

"You must charge more," Beryl Brown told him forcefully. Everyone agreed Dad should charge more. But Dad wouldn't charge more. The toy-train market wouldn't stand an increase in prices and he refused to cut down on the quality of the product by using only one topcoat of paint or leaving one carriage off the set. He had a touching faith that the public would eventually recognise the quality of the product and sales would increase to the point where he could quit factory-life for ever. But although demand never slackened, the costs of production absorbed all the profits. As winter approached the cost of heating the shed tipped the balance. The mysterious power of economics exerted its sway and the project that was to liberate him from factory oppression came to a close. He was forced to admit that the toy-trains, although successful, were not going to deliver the goods. Decisions were taken and we abandoned mass-production. The last train was packed into the last suitcase. The drilling machines and circular-saw were advertised for sale in "The Harrow Observer" and what remained of the pile of crates in the back-garden was sawn up for firewood.

But my father was resolved to escape from factory life by one means or another. He had become progressively disillusioned with his work-life. The rigid hierarchy of workers, clerical staff and management with separate canteens for each, reinforced his sense of immobility. He had no desire to become a foreman in the toolroom although offered the position a number of times. A thankless task he called it and there was no other career ladder available for toolmakers, although a very few including Ted, were offered jobs in management.

His dream was not to become a manager but to run a boarding-house by the sea when the war ended, at Hastings or Brighton or on the Devon coast. It was a utopian plan. He loved the seaside; he enjoyed meeting people; he liked food and drink and he was capable of keeping a house in good repair, fixing the plumbing and heating. It was time for a change of life when the war was over and before it was too late. It was simply a question of selling up in Rayners Lane as soon as possible and moving to the coast.

There was only one snag. My mother was against it. The boarding-house as she saw it, would involve endless cooking and bedmaking while my father chatted to the guests. The more she considered it, the more she was opposed to the whole project. "I hate housework," she said. This was certainly true. My mother's dislike of dusting and polishing was frequently articulated; she disliked ironing too and only tolerated washing because it made her hands white. Cooking was the one household skill she enjoyed but the prospect of doing that every day for a large number of people appalled her. Worst of all, though, was the housework. "Who's going to make all the beds?" she asked after one of the teatime discussions about the boarding-house project. "I don't want to spend my life making beds."

"We can employ a maid," Dad suggested but Mum was sceptical.

"Servants cost money," she declared. "You have to be businesslike to afford help."

Dad's reputation as a businessman, never very high, had sunk to a new low with the toy-train venture.

"I run a dressmaking business, I know what I'm talking

about," Mum said with authority. "I'm not going to spend the rest of my life cooking and washing up. You'll spend the time talking to guests in the bar," she said again. "I'll have to do all the hard work." Her opposition was implacable.

The boarding house dream, beloved by my father was doomed. His vision of financial independence and freedom from factory life after the war had to be financed in other ways. He tried a series of further projects: glass-topped telephone tables which held the London directories. I traipsed around the streets with him, posting handbills through the letter-boxes, but although we received about a dozen orders the venture never took off. Too few residents possessed a telephone and those who did seemed content to pile their directories on top of one another on a shelf. Only once did we receive an order from London and I accompanied him to a large office, conscious of his inferior status as he was ordered about by a man in a striped suit. The telephone tables were followed by a wire figure of a Chinese man pulling a rickshaw which held a small flowerpot, but this was undercut by a similar figure which appeared in Woolworths containing a flowering cactus for less than half the price. Escape from factory drudgery was more difficult than it appeared. Dad returned to the factory-bench with his dreams of living by the sea restricted to his annual summer-holiday.

A failure on the larger scene was the battle of Arnhem, which dominated the headlines every morning and filled the skies with thousands of gliders and 30,000 airborne troops. The paratrooper's maroon beret with the silver Pegasus became another icon as compelling to us as the Desert Rat of the Eighth Army. The plan to capture the bridges over the rivers and canals on the Dutch-German border was thwarted as the bridges were blown up before the allies arrived. The paratroopers were blown to pieces as they tried to cross the Rhine. Over a thousand paratroopers were killed and six thousand taken prisoner. Like Dunkirk it was a failure presented as a success.

We visited Portsmouth, where small boys were standing in deep mud below the pier shouting to us to throw pennies, which they scrambled for. I was fascinated by their appearance, more completely enveloped in mud than any boys I had seen before. "They're mud-larks," Dad told me. We threw them pennies then stopped at a restaurant and ate whale-meat for lunch. It looked like beefsteak and had no bones but tasted fishy. The government was encouraging us to eat whale-meat because there was a lot of it. After lunch we toured Nelson's flagship, *The Victory* and I dreamed of applying to join the navy when I was thirteen. The first step was to acquire the admiral's hat with a curving prow that I had seen in a second-hand shop in Harrow for £8. Like other visitors I read the shining brass plate on the scrubbed deck where Nelson had been shot in full-dress uniform. I marvelled at the myth and accepted it unquestionably although I later learned that more sailors had been killed under Nelson's command than under all the other commanders put together. But I lived by myths, and Nelson at Trafalgar was as important to me as the Battle of Arnhem.

29 Cobber

Because of the war the years in Rayners Lane were a time of stability. No one moved house apart from the Smarts. In contrast with the years before the war we lived in a static community with few disruptions. Most of the men had been sent away for six years; if they were in reserved occupations they worked such long hours they were rarely seen on the streets or in the homes. The women had greater independence and managed their houses, shops and schools efficiently on limited budgets and few resources. There were few changes from month to month or year to year. The streets were empty of vehicles and safe places for us in which to play marbles and cigarette-cards. Workmen rarely dug holes in the streets or pavements, no new houses or office blocks were built, no new shops opened or old ones closed. There were no ads on the billboards exhorting us to buy cars or even toothpaste. There were only the small posters put out by Ministry of Information asking us *Is Your Journey Really Necessary?* The opposite of all advertising since. There were no neon lights and hardly any traffic lights. Food was rationed and healthy, clothes endlessly mended. My mother turned sheets top to bottom, made new collars out of shirt tails and re-hemmed cuffs. Socks and stockings were always darned and my father mended my shoes on a last in the shed banging steel tips into the soles so that I clattered like a tap-dancer as I ran down the street. Nothing was wasted. Throwing anything away, apart from fish-heads wrapped in newspaper, was considered an unpatriotic act. The Squander Bug and the Litter Bug appeared on posters, unpleasant-looking beasts shaped like hairy potatoes. Apart from extravagant stories about American food-parcels there was no fresh fruit from overseas - no bananas, oranges or grapefruit. It was all very puritanical. Compared with previous decades, the war years were a stopped clock, a six-year pause while time stood still. But we could sense that the conflict was coming to an end and the clock was starting up again.

The race was on for Berlin, producing the first stirrings of rivalry between Russia and the West. The Russians, advancing swiftly from the East under Marshal Zhukov, were depicted in the newspapers as savage in their revenge against the Germans. There were stories of brutality, rape and revenge, likened to the barbarian hordes from the east sweeping across the steppes engulfing civilisation. We were light-years away from the days when we dragged our trolleys along Exeter Road collecting salvage for Uncle Joe and the Sword of Stalingrad. The power-play of international politics began to replace the certainties of war. We started to realise that the easy simplicities of conflict were not as permanent as they seemed.

Cobber and Beryl Brown had been together for several years and Cobber was a familiar sight in the small kitchenette in the Brown house with his Australian air-force sergeant's tunic slung over the back of the chair. He and Beryl had been on holiday together to Cornwall but now as the war was coming to an end, it was generally assumed that real life would start up again. Cobber would return to Australia and Ron Brown would be demobbed, as Hilda Martin's Jan would return to Poland and Mr Martin would come home and take up his old job at Harrods.

Cobber had helped us organise tug-of-war contests in the garden and showed us how to make an anchorman by tying the rope around his waist and facing the opposite way. He had helped me erect a tent for the Punch and Judy glove-puppets that Mum made so I could give a show to the alley. But now he was going.

Then came sensational news. Beryl, John and Sally would emigrate to Australia to join him when the war ended.

"Ron's the one I feel sorry for," Mrs Phipps said to Mum "fighting for his country for six years and then this happens."

"It's terrible."

"I blame her. She knew what she was doing."

"Of course she did. She led him on."

"And her husband an officer; she doesn't deserve him."

"It's a good job not everyone behaves like she does."

I knew my mother was thinking of Auntie Marjorie and Auntie Phyllis, whose husbands had been away for six years. They hadn't run off with other men. The gossip circulated up and down the alley. One afternoon Mr Brown came home in his neat blue pilot officer's uniform but after six years none of us knew him and he didn't know us. He walked about with a frown on his face and unlocked the green garage doors to inspect his car, which had been standing on wooden blocks throughout the war. Then he went away again and there was more gossip about what was going to happen.

Dad reported what Beryl Brown had said to him about her marriage on their walks from the station. "It's no good trying to go back. It's finished."

"We couldn't afford to get divorced," Mum said at one stage, "even if we wanted to." There was discussion about the cost of fares to Australia but Beryl Brown paid no attention to cost and did what she wanted to do, as she always had done.

"It's the children I feel sorry for," Mrs Phipps said.

I couldn't imagine the alley without John Brown who had been the leader of our group, the best at football, the acknowledged expert on babies and sex, the one whose house and garden were always open, the owner of the silver birch in which we constructed tree-houses.

"Cobber's going to get a divorce so they can get married," Dad reported.

"He's probably got children already," Mum said.

"He has. Two."

"What'll happen to them? What a mess."

That was the general verdict. And then there was Hilda Martin, no better than her friend Beryl but Jan departed for Poland and there was no talk of Hilda and the children following him. Nobody wanted to go to Poland. Australia meant blue skies and sandy beaches.

"I don't suppose you'll see John again", Mum said.

In the Brown hallway the trunks were packed, roped and labelled awaiting collection from Carter Paterson. Ron Brown made another visit to the house and opened the flaking blue and green corrugated iron garage doors again. The car was still inside on oil-stained wooden blocks. We stood and watched him while he knocked the blocks away and tried to start the engine by swinging it with a handle. There was a cloud of blue smoke but the engine wouldn't start. He padlocked the doors and left. The Brown house was put up for sale and the estate agent's board erected in the front garden. I couldn't imagine anyone else living in the house. It meant we wouldn't be able to play in the garden.

Then came more devastating news. A telegram suddenly arrived from Cobber's brother in Australia, saying that Cobber had been killed in a violent accident while working on a circular saw in the mill. A piece of the circular saw had snapped off and hit his head. The funeral had already taken place.

After the initial shock there were murmurings about the accident. People started to say that the telegram was probably a fake.

"Very convenient. He's gone back to his wife and kids, I expect."

"Of course."

" Beryl's a silly woman, believing all that."

"Ron won't have her back now."

"She's only herself to blame."

The divorce was going ahead and the house remained up for sale. Beryl and her children were to go to Lincolnshire where her parents lived and start a new life. It didn't make any real difference to me because they were still going away.

The alley was beginning to break up as the war came to an end. The static years were finishing as the armies entered Berlin and it seemed like nothing would ever be the same again. The Russian forces met up with the Americans on the Elbe and circled Berlin; there were rumours of Hitler's suicide and pictures of Mussolini who had been captured near Lake Como fleeing with his mistress. Mussolini and his mistress were shot and hung upside down. A woman fired five rounds into his body and screamed, "That's for each of my five sons". Every day there were executions. In France women who had slept with German officers had their hair cut off and swastikas painted on their shaven heads while crowds chased them through the streets. Unconditional surrender was the slogan. This time there would be no mercy. The Russians raised the hammer and sickle over the skeleton building of the Reichstag. The concentration camps were opened and there were pictures of bulldozers shovelling piles of stick-figures wearing black-and-white striped suits into pits. The women guards of Belsen were called wolf women.

As long as I could remember everyone had talked about the end of the war. Now it was actually happening.

My mother wanted to move house. She'd always talked about getting away from Rayners Lane. I didn't want to move, but whether I wanted to or not, I knew that I would have to. Everything was in the process of change and I didn't want anything to change. But that was impossible for me to say because the end of the war was what we had all been fighting for six years. The war had to end, but I had not anticipated the changes that would follow and were already beginning to happen. I wanted the war to end but I didn't want my life to change. I realised there was nothing I could do to stop it.

The grown-ups would do what they wanted. They would move house and take my friends away. They always did what they wanted. It was their life, not mine. They had started the war and now they were going to end it and there was nothing I could do about it.

30 Ice Cream

General Montgomery signed the surrender documents in a tent on Luneburg Heath and Admiral Doenitz surrendered to Marshal Zhukov and the American, British and French representatives. It was May 8, VE day. My father came home from work and said, "Let's go up to London." With Brian and his parents we joined an ocean of people flowing down Whitehall, the Mall, around Trafalgar Square breaking out into spasmodic dancing and cheering, shouting for the king and queen and Churchill who all duly appeared on their balconies. Everyone was deliriously happy, waving scarves and flags. We were a huge united community, dancing the okey-cokey one behind the other, arm-in-arm outside the park gates, singing the war songs of the Blitz, "She'll be Coming Round the Mountain" and "Knees Up Mother Brown" determined to stay in London until it was dark, returning home by the last Tube, feeling we had finished with war for ever and had only just begun to celebrate the glorious peace.

The festivities continued for the next two months. We went to the Victory celebrations at the Albert Hall, a triumphalist procession of all the allied nations, uniformed soldiers and sailors and airmen and nurses, spot-lit, marching down the long line of red-carpeted stairs holding their national flags while each country's national anthem played and we stood up and cheered for each one – Australia, Canada, China, France, India, New Zealand, Russia, the United States, ending with Great Britain, the architect of victory and host to the world. It was a patriotic extravaganza. Mum took me to the Victory Parade, a march-past through the streets of London. We arrived at eight o'clock in the morning – we were always five or six hours early for a kerbside seat at any royal procession, and although this was not technically royalty it counted as such. She was a little disappointed with the grey and camouflaged columns when they rolled past – tanks, armoured cars, Bren-gun carriers – but brightened up as the uniforms did - the soldiers, sailors and airmen appearing in full-dress uniforms with drums, holding their colours. We clapped and cheered the Indian regiments with their turbans, the white-helmeted marines and the Scots regiments with kilts and bagpipes. It took three hours to pass.

I bought an ice-cream, my first for six years. I could just remember the Stop Me and Buy One man before the war with a white coat and peaked cap who pedalled an ice-box along Kings Road and whose ice-creams were creamy, tasting of delicious fruits. The one I bought now was a grey warm scoop, the texture of porridge, speckled with lumps wobbling uneasily on a soft cone. Was this what I had waited six years for? Ice-creams were as colourless as the real eggs which we began to scramble, pale yellow in place of the rich, chrome yellow of the dried eggs that came out of packets.

Dad went up to London to see *The Daily Express* exhibition of photographs on the opening of the concentration camps and came back severely shaken. He could not believe the atrocities he had seen. Another, darker chapter of the war was opening, which no one had suspected. The newspapers were full of Belsen every day then Dachau, Auschwitz and Birkenau. Stories of Japanese prisoner of war camps began to fill the newspapers, with unbelievable tales of beheadings and railways of death. We knew little about the Japanese. There had been the sudden invasion of Hong Kong and the sinking of the battleship Prince of Wales by a single bomb dropped down the funnel which blew up the ammunition magazine. 50,000 people had been interned in Java but we had heard nothing about them. Apart from General Tojo, a leader we imitated by sliding a cut-up piece of orange peel under our top lips to resemble his protruding teeth, we knew the names of no other Japanese commanders. There had been the kamikaze attacks on American ships and we were familiar with the names of Iwo Jima, Okinawa and the Philippines but we are not sure where any of them were. Chamberlain had not even included Japan in his broadcast declaration of war.

Out of a cloudless blue sky the atomic bomb was dropped on Hiroshima on August 6, killing 80,000 people and flattening four square miles of the city. We realised immediately it was a new dimension of horror. A photograph in "The Daily Express" showed the outline of a body silhouetted against a stone wall with the intensity of the heat. Another bomb was dropped on Nagasaki three days later killing 40,000. The Japanese surrendered to General MacArthur in his white uniform on board an aircraft carrier. Pearl Harbour had been avenged many times over.

Science had ended the war and suddenly science was more talked about than the military. There were extensive reports of the Manhattan project and I was fascinated by a photograph of Robert Oppenheimer, a slim figure wearing a pork-pie hat striding along the streets of Los Alamos in New Mexico. He seemed a heroic figure who had made generals out of date. The word fallout entered the language and there were explanations of how the atom was split, of a mineral called uranium and heavy water. There were also sinister rumours surrounding the pilots of the planes dropping the bombs, "Little Boy" and "Fat Man," and one of them was said to have gone mad. A magic genie had escaped from the bottle in the shape of a vast, mushroom cloud that became the dominant image of our time and of the future.

VJ Day was not accompanied by the same ecstatic rejoicing as VE day. We didn't go up to London and dance the okey-cokey. The United Nations Charter was signed and there was a sombre relief that finally it was all over and we could turn our attention to the peace, but already peace was turning out to be more complicated than we had suspected.

Like my ice-cream it was not quite what I had dreamed about.

31 Miners Not Pirates

A victory party was held in Lynton Road, with a long red tablecloth over trestle tables covered with plates of homemade cakes, sandwiches, sweets and large teapots. After the tea there was a fancy-dress competition followed by games and dancing for the grown ups until midnight.

I decided to enter the fancy-dress competition, inspired by Tyrone Power in *Black Swan*, which I had watched at the Odeon Saturday morning flicks in the new technicolour, a swashbuckling drama set against the bluest of Caribbean seas. I announced my intention of going as Black Swan himself, the pirate leader. My father made a metal cutlass at work to complement my costume, the blade a throat-slitting curve, the protective shield over the handle decorated with a stamped out skull-and-crossbones. I experimented with various skin colourings, settling on a thick paste of cocoa powder, milk and water, which gave me a fierce, mulatto pirate-tan. I tied a triangle of crimson silk around my head, hung large brass curtain rings on my ears and wore a torn white shirt that billowed out like a galleon sail. To complete the picture I wound a broad red sash around my waist, decorated my face with a burned cork moustache and held a kitchen knife between my teeth. Surveying myself in the mirror I felt Black Swan himself would have envied my appearance.

John Brown appeared forlornly in our kitchen doorway as I was putting the finishing touches to my brilliant costume.

"What are you going as?" I asked.

"Dunno", he said. He had a grizzled look on his face but I felt no sympathy for him and continued preening myself with the callousness we exhibited towards each other on such occasions. His mother was out at work and his father still in the RAF.

"Come on, we'll find something for you," my father said and

led him down to the shed, from which he emerged fifteen minutes later as a miner, his face covered in coal dust, a pair of my father's baggy trousers tied with string below his knees, a helmet with a torch taped on top, holding a pickaxe and a miner's lamp made of a cocoa tin with a strip of gauze and a candle inside.

"The Bevin Boy," Dad explained.

I was unconcerned. His outfit had obviously been thrown together at the last minute and he looked grimy and disreputable. He was not in the same sartorial class as a pirate.

After the tea the fancy-dress competition took place and some twenty of us paraded in front of the judges who went into a huddle by the teapots. The senior judge stood up with a sheet of paper in his hand.

"Third prize, the fairy," he announced. There was loud applause from the surrounding parents and comments on how pretty four-year old Shirley from Lulworth Crescent looked.

"Second, the Land Army Girl." This was Sally Farmer, dressed in britches with a yellow headscarf. There was more cheering and clapping, especially from the women. Then there was a long pause.

"First prize, the Bevin Boy," the judge announced, and John Brown, with a big grin on his face, held up his lantern. There was prolonged cheering and clapping. I couldn't believe it. They must all have gone mad. How could anybody in their right mind prefer a miner to a pirate? Or a Land Army girl? Or – most humiliating of all – a stupid fairy with gauze wings? I was not even second or third. Black Swan had been totally ignored.

"It's because Bevin Boys are topical," Dad said, trying to comfort me. I had difficulty not bursting into tears. Not only was it unfair, but my father was guilty of treachery - he must have known what the judges would choose and he had deliberately not told me. Topical was not a word I was familiar with but now I knew it would stick in my mind for ever. I wanted nothing more to do with the metal cutlass and plunged it into the front hedge and left it there. I didn't care, I desperately told myself. What could be more boring than a stupid Bevin Boy? But I also realised with a sinking, hopeless feeling that miners were part of a different post-war world. Pirates were not as important as miners to grown-ups; miners were the new heroes not pirates.

I tried to conceal my feelings for the rest of the afternoon. There were games for children, then grown-up games. In one contest Dad raced for the same chair as Beryl Brown, who got there first and collapsed onto the road, legs and skirts flying in the air. As it grew dark there was dancing with music from a gramophone, playing waltzes and quicksteps in an upstairs window. My father and mother glided around in the road. "Your mum and dad are the best dancers in the street," Lena Hartel told me, as the moon rose and the lamps came on.

I was proud for them although it didn't make up for Black Swan's defeat by a Bevin Boy.

32 *Losses*

Fifty million people were killed in the war: twenty million Russians, ten million Chinese, five million Germans, five million Poles, two million Japanese and a million Jugoslavs. In India four million people died as a result of famine caused by the war. The French and Americans lost half a million, the British three hundred thousand. More than half of the dead were civilians.

Bob was put to sleep and I was heartbroken. He had been my confidant, sitting on the mat by the kitchen door listening to me with his sympathetic brown eyes and his tongue lolling out, seeming to understand everything I told him. Bob was more beautiful than anyone else I knew. He had a handsome head and a coat of brown and white curls with a smell that was comforting and reassuring. I used to bury my nose in his coat and sniff him. He had been there, patient and eternal, since before I could remember. In his younger days on walks near the river Colne at Rickmansworth, I would throw a stick in the river and he would leap in to retrieve it, his head pushing through the water with the stick in his mouth, making a V-shaped wave then scrambling up the bank to shake himself over everyone. He sat with me outside the pub at Sarratt when the grown-ups went inside and left me with a bag of crisps and a bottle of lemonade. He never growled or showed anger. He was always pleased to see me, his short tail thumping on the mat. I would brush his curls until they shone, and once, when a tin of white paint fell on him as Dad was painting the house, I combed out the lumps of paint for weeks afterwards, while he sat there, uncomplaining and unresentful. When I was younger I had ridden on his back but he had become fat and waddled about with his tongue hanging out. He would eat porridge and everything else that was offered to him. He lost his game-dog elegance and spent longer on the mat, suffering in the heat of summer. Now he was gone for ever.

My father was upset by the loss of Bob too. He had lost his night-time walking companion and cried when he returned from the vet's without him. I was not consulted or informed about Bob's disappearance. He simply vanished without explanation.

My bear, Cubby, vanished in similar manner and at about the same time. I had slept with Cubby all my life. His blue hair was almost scuffed off and there were bald patches on his stomach and back but like Bob, he was an inseparable companion, always on my pillow with a fidelity I took for granted. Suddenly there was only the blank whiteness of the pillow like a snowfield.

I did not enquire about his disappearance. It was something I did not wish to broach with the grown-up world because I knew what the answer would be. "You're much too old for a teddy bear." A judgement had been made that was beyond my power to change as it had been decided that Bob was too old to continue living. Like Bob, he was loved, especially at night when he was my companion against creaking stairs and crouching intruders. I drifted off to sleep with him pressed against my chest. Now there was only myself to sleep with and no Bob to tell secrets to. It was a bleaker existence.

Father Christmas also disappeared completely. Michael informed me on one of his visits that he didn't exist and that the whole story was an elaborate concoction on the part of the grown-ups. He assumed that I had known for years that Father Christmas was a grown-up fabrication and that he was merely restating an accepted fact. I was shattered but I went along with his grim news and pretended that it was already known to me because I was clearly too old to believe in such things as I was too old to have a teddy bear. To continue to believe in Father Christmas was childish.

"I knew that," I said.

But if Father Christmas didn't exist how had I been so completely fooled for years? I had been taken to shake hands with him in Sopers department store in Harrow and although I never believed there were reindeers pulling sledges through the sky my ardent faith had transcended such literal details. If he wasn't true, what else might be called into question? I assumed a mature indifference to hide my loss. My father had made the forts and the sewing-machines - I knew that but there were many inexplicable things in the world and Father Christmas's relationship with presents and my parents was not something that was more mysterious than many others. What hurt was the knowledge that I had been lied to for years and I felt resentful; a part of me would never believe grown-ups so completely ever again. They were obviously capable of deceit over a long period - all my lifetime in fact. What else had they lied about?

John Brown produced a condom, dangling it in the air in front of us. "Do you know what this is?" he asked.

I thought it was a balloon.

This was greeted with a knowing smirk.

"No, it's a spunk bag," he announced, "the man puts it over his tool before he puts his tool into the lady. It's to stop them having a baby."

This was too much information for me, coming as it did on top of the Father Christmas collapse. I felt my world was caving in.

"I found it over the fields," John Brown went on. "It's where they go to shag."

I realised my lack of knowledge was devastating. What John Brown was saying seemed another flight of absurd fantasy but on the other hand John Brown was the acknowledged expert on all matters sexual and always had been. He was our oracle of forbidden information, but in spite of this I felt impelled to question him.

"How do you know?"

He swung his evidence back and forth.

"See, that's where the spunk goes," he said, squeezing the condom so that the liquid inside it – whatever it was – bulged ominously into the teat at the end. There were too many questions to ask. Unlike Father Christmas, who had disappeared leaving a vacuum, this new revelation ushered in a universe of further enquiry.

But I felt disinclined to continue.

"That's what your Dad and Mum do," John Brown continued. That was something else I didn't want to think about. It was inconceivable that my parents would have anything to do with such things; certainly they didn't go shagging over the fields where we collected frogspawn. It was impossible to imagine my parents using the rubbery thing John Brown was dangling up and down in front of us.

"They're Durex," he informed us. "You buy them in packets of three at the barber's."

"I've never seen them."

"You haven't looked. They're next to the mirror behind the green bottles of hair-oil."

I remembered the green bottles of hair-oil but why would they be there? What did having babies have to do with hair-oil and the barber's? Was there some connection I'd missed? One part of me didn't want to know any more about SB's as he called them but another part of me wanted to know everything. John Brown, however, had exhausted his fund of information. The condom was his great exhibit and it was not until some time later when Brian discovered "Sexual Techniques for Married Couples" underneath the ironed sheets at the top of his parents' wardrobe that we were able to pursue our research. Meanwhile the condom was real enough and the precursor to others we found scattered over the fields. It had many of the qualities of the grown-up world – colourless and heavy and rubbery. It clearly wasn't a balloon. It wasn't as much fun and it seemed to have less to do with parties than with an ominous future which I would have to engage with in the coming post-war years whether I wanted to or not.

33   11 Plus

I was in D4, the top class at Roxbourne, which in its anti-elitist enthusiasm had decided to reverse the accepted categories and make A1 the bottom group in the school. Miss Drew was the class mistress for D4, a formidable, silver-haired middle-aged woman with bulging forearms whose method of punishment was to bunch her fist and swing it like a pendulum against the back of a recalcitrant pupil, propelling him (it was invariably a he) towards the blackboard at the front of the class. Miss Drew stood for no nonsense and was in no doubt that her pedagogy was a successful one. Every morning after we had sung a hymn about how we ploughed the fields and scattered the good seed on the land, Miss Drew would take us for Mental Arithmetic standing in front of the class with her large arms crossed in front of her as a warning to the inattentive and the idle.

"What will five and a half pounds of tomatoes cost at threepence a pound?" she demanded. We were given two minutes to compute this and to write the answer down on a numbered sheet of paper. "How long will it take to fill a 200 gallon swimming pool if the pipe pumps eight gallons a minute?" Miss Drew proceeded. The penalty for slowness, poor hearing or wrong answers was to be punched on the spine by Miss Drew's clenched fist at a velocity of about sixty miles an hour. Miss Drew was a dedicated teacher who regarded D4 as her personal fiefdom; she prowled between the desks like a lioness, cuffing pupils who had failed to catch the details of the mental arithmetic problem or whose pencil was not properly sharpened. Miss Drew had her favourites, all girls, who habitually occupied the first ten places in the class order and whose hands shot up to answer her questions with an alacrity that seemed to us boys disturbing and treacherous. At times the class threatened to become a dialogue between Miss Drew and Shirley Richardson, a small girl in a red cardigan with pigtail plaits and glasses who consistently came top of the class and was so far advanced in knowledge and enthusiasm that it scarcely seemed worth bothering to compete with her.

But Miss Drew did not allow us to congregate at the back of the class and dip the girls' plaits into inkwells. We were under close surveillance and our essays and sums were continuously assessed with Miss Drew's red pen and an array of gold and silver stars or blue and green spots which appeared every day in our exercise books as indicators of our intellectual progress.

Then one afternoon Mr Harvey appeared. Why he did so was a mystery. We were not told and we didn't ask, for the replacement of Miss Drew was a stroke of fortune that we did not wish to threaten. Mr Harvey was a dashingly handsome young man who had served as a pilot officer in the Fleet Air Arm and whose notion of teaching was to explain in fascinating detail the missions he had flown. He covered the blackboard with elaborate diagrams of radar beams and fuselages and talked about the raids he had taken part in. We were captivated and questioned him with genuine curiosity about his adventures. For a week we discussed the battles for Malta and Crete, U-boats and depth charges and the difficulties of landing on an aircraft-carrier in a force seven gale. Young Mr Harvey was eloquent and enthusiastic and treated us as if we were civilised human beings. He enjoyed our attention and we adored him.

Then one morning the following week Miss Drew reappeared to reclaim her class. Mr Harvey was never seen again. " You don't appear to have learned anything" Miss Drew informed us acidly, "I don't know how you're ever going to pass the examination."

·But we were loyal to our hero. Not a word was uttered which might suggest that Mr Harvey's teaching skills were not of the finest. He had come and gone over the distant horizon like one of his silver-bodied planes and we never forgot him.

Miss Drew proceeded to launch into an intensive campaign to make up for the days wasted by Mr Harvey, talking more and more about the exam. What exam was this? We had no idea what an exam was. One afternoon as we were about to go home, she produced a sheaf of papers with the three curved scimitars of Middlesex County Council emblazoned on the front. "Give these to your parents," she commanded us. Our parents would select which school they wished us to attend in the event of our passing the examination that was now being referred to as the eleven-plus.

Our knowledge of what was to be a watershed in our lives was as meagre as our preparation for it. We were aware that the pupils at Harrow County wore dark blue blazers and the pupils at Pinner County wore brown blazers with a gold stag on the pocket, but apart from the design of the blazers no other information was available on which a rational choice might be made. Harrow County was popularly regarded as superior to Pinner County but nobody quite knew why. My father, never averse to undertaking research with discussion groups in the toolroom, took the papers into work and returned in the evening with the startling news that the schools whose names were printed in bold typeface under the heading of Independent Grammar Schools were superior even to Harrow County, and of this small group, Merchant Taylors' School was the best and the one I should aim for.

My mother's attention picked up at the mention of Merchant Taylors for it clearly had something to do with tailoring and dressmaking. Subsequent research however, established that it was not a trade school but an institution similar to Cooper's School that Uncle Norman had attended in Bow, founded by a London livery company that was no more associated with sewing gentlemen's suits than Coopers was with making beer-barrels. Mum's interest was sustained however. Merchant Taylors', whatever its associations with tailoring, was a fee-paying school, a public school. After further discussions it was unanimously decided that it should definitely be our collective choice.

But the examination had still to be passed.

On the appointed day we waited in line outside the school

lavatories, fluttering our hands underneath our jerseys in imitation of our palpitating hearts, although we were not genuinely apprehensive having so little idea of what awaited us. Finally the doors were opened and we were allowed inside. The white booklets lay folded on our desks looking important and official with printed writing on the covers. We were instructed not to touch them until Miss Drew gave the word. I realised it was like a race. We read the instructions on the cover and then, at Miss Drew's command, "Start now!" opened them like large white butterflies. I discovered that it was the English paper, the first of three, and that I was required to write an essay about a foreign country I should like to visit and explain why I wanted to go there.

I took a deep breath. Foreign countries were not high on my list of priorities. I had never been to one and knew little about them, apart from what I had heard and read during the six years of war. This, I realised fairly quickly, was not a great help. What did I really know about France or Italy in spite of my reading about them in "The Daily Express" for the past six years? Practically nothing; war was an inadequate source of information and I knew as much about the West Indies from the placards dangling in Lakins as I did about the countries of Europe in which we had been fighting. Nor did I want to go there from the pictures of shell-torn villages I had seen. I tinkered with the idea of Switzerland, where I imagined myself skiing down the slopes of the Matterhorn, twisting through dark pine-forests past wooden chalets. But I realised that was about the beginning and end of my knowledge of Swiss culture and was not likely to impress the examiners. We had not been taught anything about Switzerland, or any other country for that matter. Geography as a separate subject had not existed and I sat chewing the end of my pen searching desperately for inspiration when it descended on me if not from Heaven, at least from a closely related source. I remembered the Holy Land or Palestine, that mystical country illustrated in pink and yellow maps at the back of my bible which I had been hearing about continuously since I was five years old. I had little desire to visit the Holy Land but that was irrelevant. The important fact was that I knew a lot about it, certainly more than I did about Switzerland. Between skiing in Switzerland and walking around the Holy Land there was no competition. I launched into a heartfelt account of my desire to visit Bethlehem, the Mount of Olives, Jerusalem, Calvary, the Dead Sea and anywhere else I could think of that would assist my religious and literary pilgrimage. There was even the Old Testament that could be plundered – the walls of Jericho, Caanan and the Red Sea. I was surprised to discover how much I remembered from my Sunday afternoons with the Christian Brethren and church parades with the Baptists. I was a fund of information about lost sheep, good Samaritans and foolish virgins. I allowed myself dramatic moments with the Garden of Gethsemane and the Road to Damascus and when I laid down my pen I felt a sincere if hypocritical satisfaction in having covered so much ground in the Holy Land, a place I now felt more benign towards than ever before and which one day, I might even consider visiting. Such was my power of self-persuasion.

The following day was the arithmetic paper which Miss Drew had prepared us for with her back-thwacking morning routine of questions. But arithmetic was not my strong subject and although I was capable of dividing and multiplying and even of elementary percentages, I had little idea what the factors of 51 might be and no idea about how to set about finding them. Only after we came out of the exam did I discover that 17 and 3 were the correct answers, and that I had been familiar with them from my Sunday evening darts games where treble seventeen had been an automatic score I had known from my earliest years.

But it was the third paper, General Knowledge, that proved the most calamitous and convinced me I had fallen down the elephant-pit of failure. There were puzzling diagrams of Scottish kilts with missing oblongs and underneath a range of kilt patterns, one of which I was required to select to fill the missing space. These were followed by sequences of squiggles and curves in boxes, which I was required to add to by placing similar squiggles and curves in empty boxes. I had never met exercises like this before and they seemed bizarre and confusing. Slightly more familiar was a paragraph about Tom being taller than George but shorter than Henry who was taller than Fred. This information was followed by a series of statements about their respective heights which I was asked to classify as true or false. Then there were baffling lines of letters, A E F H..... where I was asked to supply the next in the sequence with no guidance apart from my knowledge of the alphabet.

After an hour of this I began to feel distinctly woozy and retraced my steps through the questions, altering almost every one of my answers and then losing confidence in my alterations. What did they want? The whole paper started to swim in front of me as I realised that either my original answers were wrong or my alterations were wrong. It seemed a precarious performance and I felt I had lost my bearings completely and was wandering without a compass in completely strange territory. But somehow I passed. So did Henry Goldberg who had also elected to go to Merchant Taylors' and John Brown who had opted for Pinner County but was destined for Lincolnshire once the divorce came through. John Martin disappeared into a fee-paying school that was planned to lead him towards being a doctor. Only Brian, my closest friend, had failed.

"Poor Brian," Mum said. Brian would have to spend the rest of his school life at Eastcote Lane Sec Mod next to the fish-and-chip shop until he was fifteen when he would leave and seek employment as a plumber's mate or garage mechanic. He came round to see me and shrugged his shoulders. We would all be scattered to the four winds. But I was excited at passing and could only think of a glittering future that had suddenly opened out without my doing very much at all.

34 The Interview

My parents and I were summoned to attend an interview at Merchant Taylors' School in Moor Park and my father took the day off work. We dressed in our Sunday best and began the momentous journey from Rayners Lane to North Harrow, then by train to Moor Park followed by a walk through a small woodland copse and along a road to tall wrought iron gates decorated with the school motto, *Concordia Parvae Res Crescunt*, which I subsequently discovered meant little things grow great together. And there, a mile away across a sea of green grass, on which dozens of boys in white flannels were playing games of cricket watched by others lying in the shade of the trees, the school was visible like a ship on the horizon. Overawed we began walking up the long drive as shining cars drove past us.

"It's a long way to come each day," Dad said. "It'll be good exercise."

We walked along in silence until we reached the clock tower where there was a master waiting to meet us, clothed in a long black gown which opened out behind him as he strode swiftly away with my parents, leaving me in the care of a grey-suited boy who led me up stairs and along corridors lined with photographs of Greek buildings and Greek sculptures. I followed meekly, climbing the squeaking wooden stairs to the library where another gowned master with a reddish face and glasses was seated at a table holding a photograph in front of him. He shook my hand and I sat opposite him.

"Perhaps you would look at this," he instructed me without any further discussion.

It was a photograph of an aircraft factory. There were workers climbing ladders and standing on the wings of partially constructed planes. On the floor were engines that other men were inspecting. I stared at it for several minutes until my examiner whisked it away and placed it face down on the table.

"Now describe it to me," he commanded. It seemed a familiar scene, although I had never been inside an aircraft factory. I had little difficulty recalling it, including the name of the firm written along the upright of the ladder in small letters, a detail that seemed to impress my examiner more than it deserved. Next he produced a square of cardboard cut into eight or nine sections which he proceeded to shuffle about on the surface of the table. "Now reassemble these into a square," he ordered. It was not as complicated as similar puzzles I had encountered and I managed it after several minutes.

"Which books have you read lately?" he asked. I mentioned Kipling's *Jungle Book* and the William books by Richmal Crompton which I had recently discovered and was reading passionately and threw in John Bunyan's *Pilgrims Progress* for good measure, on the same basis as I had written my essay on my desire to visit to the Holy Land.

"Which clubs or societies have you joined?"

I gave an edited version of my involvement with the Cubs and Sunday School, explaining my reading from Isaiah as though it had been a valuable and interesting experience. The interview concluded, he stood up and shook my hand; I noticed there was a smell of tobacco from his jacket and gown and that his forefinger was stained bright yellow.

The boy who had led me up to the library reappeared and I was told to follow him down the squeaking stairs to where my parents were waiting. We walked back along the drive where the boys were still lying under the trees watching cricket in the sunlight.

"I had to promise that you'd join the Army Cadet Corps when you are fourteen if they accept you," Dad said. "Of course I said yes. They seem very proud of their cadet force." I felt sorry for my father having to agree about the cadet force because I knew he didn't like uniforms or war.

"The headmaster seems a very nice man," Mum said.

A week later a letter in a thick, cream envelope addressed to me arrived. It had a dark blue embossed coat of arms at the top, showing two camels holding up a shield with three tents on it.

I could hardly bear to open it and my hands were shaking as I did so. I had been accepted and was to start in September as a day boy. My parents were overjoyed. I tried to pretend that I was not especially thrilled when talking with them but when I was alone, I allowed myself to go into spasms of excitement.

My world was going to change for ever. There was an immediate flurry of preparations and endless speculation on the exclusive nature of the school. Long typed lists were sent stating that I was to wear a No 77 Daniel Neal's grey flannel suit, a white shirt with a detachable collar and collar-studs, house tie, a black school cap adorned with a silver lamb holding a flag, black shoes and in winter black and white striped scarf. My games kit was to include rugby shirts, shorts and boots, cricket flannels and a blazer, with a straw boater as an optional extra.

"I don't know how we're going to manage financially," Mum said.

I was presented with a Norman two-wheeled bicycle for my achievement, which was rapidly becoming the centre of neighbourhood and family discussions. "It's a very good school," everyone said. "Which side of the family does he get his brains from?" was a topic of frequent speculation with the honours divided between Uncle Norman and Mum's family. "It's a chance we never had" was the universal comment. I realised I was part of the new post-war era, sent to a public school by a Labour government that was committed to paying for everything except my lunches, school uniform and sports-clothes. There was a report in the Harrow Observer where I saw my name in print for the first time. I was a neighbourhood success.

Brian came to see me. I was embarrassed to detail all my plans and arrangements for the new school; a gap had opened up but we weren't going to talk about it. We continued to make our arrangements as if nothing had intervened to separate our lives.

It never occurred to any of us to question the judgement of those authorities who classified Brian and me with such certainty and who sifted what they regarded as the wheat from the chaff with such a consummate sense of their own infallibility.

It was no more thinkable that we should question the

educational experts that than it was to argue with Miss Drew about how long it took a pipe pumping eight gallons a minute to fill a 200 gallon swimming pool.

We all knew there were certain indisputable facts in life and the rightness of the decisions taken by those in authority was one of them.

35   Circumcision of the Heart

"Way!"
"Why."
"Way!"
"Why!"
"Way."
"Come out to the front Daniel!"

It was the Divinity class, taken by the headmaster, Mr Elder. We were studying the circumcision of the heart from St. Paul's letter to the Galatians, an intellectual argument that seemed of greater interest to Mr Elder than it did to the rest of us but this was not Mr Elder's immediate concern.

"The *way* to salvation," expostulated Mr Elder, who was as new to the school as I was and had come from Scotland as his strong Scottish accent indicated. "Not the *why* to salvation!"

I stood despairingly in front of the class.

"Say after me: the *way* to salvation!"

"The *whey* to salvation!"

"That's better. Keep saying it."

"The *whey* to salvation, the *whey* to salvation, the *whey* to salvation!"

I remembered doing this once before with *Geography* at Roxbourne, but this time it was different: this was an onslaught on my accent which encompassed every word I spoke in my suburban north London dialect. *Way/why* was only this morning's target. It could be any word at any time. I had already been indicted for the glottal stop in *film* and *milk bottle* and spent some time in practising lifting my tongue off the floor of my mouth; I had been ridiculed for saying, *"He didn't ought to be in the team"*, which seemed to me a perfectly correct use of grammar and publicly castigated for saying *laying* instead of *lying*. It was unnerving. I was conscious that I was becoming too terrified to say anything. I had always been fearful of opening my mouth to sing, but now I was scared of opening my mouth to speak.

It wasn't only pronunciation and syntax that was inadmissible but my vocabulary as well. "When is it playtime?" I had asked Mr Dutton, our form master at the start of term. His lip curled in disgust. "We don't call it playtime," he sneered. "We call it The Quarter here. Don't let me hear you call it playtime again."

I was in the Third Form, a new class especially constituted for the ten boys from Middlesex and five from Hertfordshire selected by the state, plus ten fee-paying boys to give it respectability. The Third Form was the school's first concession to state education and the shock waves were still being felt.

I seemed to be unsuccessful at every subject except History, where I discovered a facility for drawing medieval siege instruments and Norman soldiers in suits of chain-mail. Even here I had fallen foul of the history master, Mr Baiss, who said to me one morning, "You don't seem to be good at any subject except mine." I felt this was a below the belt comment, since I *was* good at his subject and his remark revealed that he had been talking about me with the teachers of other subjects.

Apart from History I seemed to be incapable of understanding anything. Mathematics was turning into a sea of incomprehensible facts in which I was in danger of drowning. Mr Parsons, the teacher who had interviewed me with the photograph of the aircraft-factory, seemed less impressed with my knowledge of compound fractions than he had been with my memory of the aircraft-factory. His teaching method was to stand on the dais at the front of the class and avoid eye-contact with his pupils while delivering a mathematical monologue to the opposite wall. As there was no possibility of halting his flow of information, I sensed my hold on the subject slipping as he moved from one concept to the next, leaving me floundering in his wake. Mr Parsons did not encourage questions and as he moved on I realised that certain basic mathematical concepts were being left behind and that I should never be able to catch up.

Latin too was becoming impenetrable, although I had started with considerable excitement, chanting the declensions from my Latin primer half-aloud on top of the 230 bus as it took me homeward from North Harrow station to Rayners Lane. "*Puella, puellam, puellae,*" I murmured to myself in mantra-fashion. There was something therapeutic about declining Latin nouns, "*Puellae, puellae, puellarum*". In my new intoxication I decide to launch into Latin poetry inspired by Macaulay's *The Lays of Ancient Rome,* a poem I had recently discovered and opening lines of which I knew by heart:

>*Lars Porsena of Clusium*
>*By the nine gods he swore,*
>*The great House of Tarquin*
>*Should suffer wrong no more.*

Into this hypnotic rhythm I tried to weave the meagre lexicon of my Latin primer penning some dozen lines of the words I had learned so far. I showed them with some pride to Mr Cherrett, the Latin teacher, who took the opportunity to deliver an address on the correct nature of Latin scansion, "We do not rhyme like this in Latin, Daniel. Classical verse moves by quantity, not by syllable. I'm afraid you have completely the wrong end of the stick. Don't try to run before you can walk."

This encouragement heralded the end of my career as a Latin poet and my involvement with Latin prose was not much more successful. I found it difficult to unscramble the knots into which Latin seemed to writhe like a wounded snake. I gradually became alienated from the Romans and whatever it was they were trying to tell me about their villas or the invasion of Gaul. There was clearly something congenitally wrong with me. It was a mistake that I had ever been allowed to pass the eleven-plus.

French was equally catastrophic in its own way. Mr Dutton, our form master, had launched a pedagogic experiment by teaching us the phonetic alphabet *ab initio* so that we would possess a solid foundation on which to build our linguistic competence. Unfortunately he neglected to explain to us that French was not written in phonetic symbols and I assumed it was a language akin to Arabic or Hindu, written with a variety of squiggles and flourishes. It was only after six months that I discovered French words were spelled with the same letters as English. We spent hours intoning the nasal sounds and trilling r's, feats I was unable to perform with the necessary competence.

And when I proudly informed Mrs Smart that I was learning French and showed her the linguistic symbol for *chat*, she was mystified, feeling that this was not her native language as she knew it.

Geography, like History, was taught by Mr Baiss from a book chiefly remarkable for its ink-blotted pages and out-of-focus black and white photographs of women with headscarves picking tea in Ceylon. Interspersed with these images were line-drawings of ox-bow lakes and interlocking spurs. I was not captivated by Geography except for colouring blue sea around the edges of islands and as a result sank even further in Mr Baiss's estimation.

I enjoyed songs but was aware that accurate musical sounds and notation were beyond my skill. Mr Tomblings, the music teacher, struck a note on the piano, asked me to sing it and when he heard the result shunted me to one side where I joined the crowd of rejects on the musical scrap-heap. Music lessons were held in an attic room where the walls were painted with half-finished murals of band stands and the ceiling was full of holes where tone-deaf pupils had poked their fingers into the soundproofing, a muted, windowless cube that did little for my musical education.

Gym was another ordeal: I found climbing ropes almost impossible and leaping over wooden horses a dangerous practice. My body seemed too gangly to swing over bars and too tall to squat cross-legged with my knees flat on the floor as required by Mr Brown the gym master who had his acolytes – nimble, fair-haired boys whose locks he stroked and whose bottoms he caressed. I was too unappealing to be cosseted in this way. My troubles were more mundane: I found the process of undressing and dressing at high speed fraught with difficulty and was usually the last to leave, struggling to pull my collar on to the collar-stud as I rushed out, with my tie untied, shoelaces undone and shirt hanging out of my trousers.

Art was the only subject in which I was not subject to criticism. I splashed about with the poster paints on blue sugar paper, painting a rendition of Black Swan on his pirate galleon surrounded by blue smoke and cannonballs of fire. Mr Witney was not prescriptive and we were allowed a large measure of freedom. I enjoyed carpentry too, although this was conducted by Mr Damon with military precision and discipline. Planes had to be held in the correct manner; chisels carefully sharpened, benches swept from left to right. Every tool had to be replaced in its correct position. We began our carpentry curriculum with a lapped-halving joint, progressed to mortise and tenon, then on to

toothbrush rack, key ring holder and teapot-stand, ending with an inlaid chessboard of sycamore and mahogany. It was work I enjoyed but Mr Damon was not a man given to the pleasure-principle and as neither art nor carpentry were held in high esteem by the school authorities my success in these areas brought me little prestige. I felt myself sinking gradually down to the bottom of the class in competence, confidence and reputation.

The grim truth, I decided, was that I lacked not only intelligence but physical agility and dexterity. I was clumsy and incapable of understanding mathematics or pronouncing foreign languages or unravelling dead ones. I couldn't even trill an "r". I was no good at games and was attracting the hostility of those who ran the place. I was constantly in trouble with the monitors, senior boys with green striped ties, and the prompters, who wore red striped ones. Both patrolled the corridors and grounds as part of their duties in search of malefactors. A week never went by when I was not given a hundred lines, forty letters to the line, for not wearing my cap properly, for having my hands in my pockets, for sitting on the radiators where only the sixth formers were allowed to sit, for talking in prayers, for running down the corridor, for walking on the grass, for wearing my tie at the wrong angle or for writing the previous hundred lines in a slovenly fashion. I felt trapped, defeated and in despair.

Mr Baiss considered he would assist my development by caning me as a corrective for what he conceived to be my general degeneracy. He summoned me to stay after class and after delivering a short talk on the school, its traditions and the need to uphold them, he lifted the lid of his desk, took out a length of bamboo cane and bent it backwards and forwards in the classic manner in front of me. I seemed not to want to fit in, he said, not to want to take advantages of all the opportunities that the school had to offer. Mr Baiss had thick lips and I disliked him but in spite of this I felt there was considerable truth in what he was saying. He was right and I was wrong. He was going to cane me to show me that the school was not to be trifled with and that it was a serious place where I must apply myself seriously or take the consequences. Did I understand? He then instructed me to lean over the front desk, lifted the tail of my jacket and began to hit me with the cane, pausing between each stroke. It was the first time I had been hit with a stick. I gritted my teeth and clung to the far side of the lid, determined not to yell but aware that he was hitting me as hard as he could. He hit me six times, breathing heavily, then said, "You can go now." I staggered out.

In spite of Mr Baiss's efforts I still seemed unable to make myself liked by those in charge. A few weeks later, five of us were scrimmaging in the classroom when Mr Dutton walked in and demanded that we see him after the class. He offered us the choice of fifty lines or the cane.

"Fifty lines sir," each one of my co-delinquents replied, as Mr Dutton walked along the row. It was perhaps a theatrical impulse based on memories of a film I had seen, where French resistance workers were lined up by the Gestapo, that made me say, "The cane, sir." Mr Dutton laid into me as if choosing the cane in itself was a form of insubordination, as perhaps it was.

There was very little I enjoyed in my first term. Sometimes I would stop and wonder how I would get through the next seven years which stretched into the endless distance. There were elements of rugby I liked: the cold mud of the field followed by the hot bathwater in the long tiled troughs, the satisfyingly aching bruises as I trudged home in the November greyness. And there were the reproductions of paintings in the Third Form classroom that I stared at for hours when I had given up hope of pleasing Mr Dutton with my understanding of phonetics or French pronunciation: Rembrandt's *Man in a Gold Helmet*, his high Spanish helmet embossed in gold disappearing magically into the darkness; Vermeer's *Girl in Ermine*, holding a bead necklace proudly in front of her; De Hooch's *Card-players*, with the black-and-white tiled floor and the cavalier with his plumed hat holding up a wine glass to the light and, on the back wall, Holbein's *Merchant in the Steelyard*, with his inkwell and piles of coins on a thick Turkish carpet, every detail hypnotically fascinating.

These were my real instructors, beautiful and wordless.

36 Guilty Men

The Nuremberg War Trials were held. There were photographs showing white-helmeted, white-gaitered American police in the panelled courtroom, with Hess, Goering, Doenitz and others sitting in long rows in the dock.

But the main actors were absent. Hitler was reputedly dead with Eva Braun, shot in his Berlin bunker, although there were rumours that he was still alive; Goebbels had killed himself and his wife and family of six children; Himmler committed suicide in poison before the trial opened and Goering, the chief representative of what remained of the Reich, swallowed a cyanide capsule he had smuggled into the prison the night before he was due to be hanged. Hess sat alone and uncommunicative. All the major criminals were gone. We felt we had been cheated.

But it was the country that was on trial as much as individuals and everyone believed that Germany was collectively guilty. The photographs of the death camps proved the country's guilt beyond any doubt and the plea that the accused were only obeying orders was never accepted, although obedience to orders had traditionally formed the basis for every army in history. Nor was there any right of appeal. Only much later was this challenged.

Germany's guilt was absolute although racism itself was not on trial and was not a concept we were familiar with. The government of the United States, the organiser of the Nuremberg trials, maintained a segregated army abroad and a system of discrimination amounting to apartheid in many states at home with separate drinking fountains and lavatories for black

Americans and separate seats for blacks at the back of every bus that ran through Washington, the nation's capital. Americans of Japanese descent had also been persecuted although we did not know this. Two thirds of the 127,000 living in the States had been born in the US, yet in 1942 President Roosevelt ordered them to move from California to camps in the desert, and two years later the Supreme Court ruled that the evacuation was constitutional. The Japanese Americans were compelled to sell their homes at low prices and forced to work harvesting crops in the fields, returning to their barracks in barbed wire compounds every night.

The British had their racism too. Survivors of the Japanese camps in Singapore, Hong Kong and Java were paid £10,000 each after their five-year imprisonment, providing they were able to prove that their grandparents were British. If not, the fact that they had been imprisoned as British was discounted. But we were not told about this either. The Gurkha soldiers were paid less proportionately for their military pensions than British soldiers. There was apartheid in British South Africa, India and other British colonies. Genocide, perhaps the chief justification for the Second World War in retrospect, was not the chief reason for going to war. But this was not debated and genocide, like racism was not a familiar concept.

On St. Barnabas' Day, the members of the Worshipful Company of Merchant Taylors, wearing long, ermine fringed cloaks, attended a service in the Great Hall, holding small nosegays of flowers to ward off infection from the plague. The school was founded in 1561 by Sir Thomas White for merchants' sons; it was described as a grammar school in the original documents but Mr Elder made it clear on frequent occasions that we were not a grammar school and had little in common with such institutions. Merchant Taylors was on Mr Gladstone's celebrated list of nine public schools, which was regarded as definitive. We wore suits and went to school on Saturdays. I discovered that there was another Merchant Taylors' School in Lancashire, founded at the same time by the same company for the same purpose, but this institution threatened our uniqueness and I was told never to mention it again.

The first headmaster, Richard Mulcaster, was a man with Renaissance ideas on the teaching of English as a creative medium as well as conventional Greek and Latin. His illustrious pupils included the poet Edmund Spenser, six translators of the Authorised Version of the Bible, the chief physicians to Queen Elizabeth and James 1, Thomas Lodge, the pamphleteer and Thomas Kyd, the author of *The Spanish Tragedy*, the most popular play of its time.

Such glories were long gone. Mr Elder's chief enthusiasms, were for the army cadet corps, divinity classes, Gilbert and Sullivan and the novels of John Buchan. The cadet force was an institutional obsession with parades every Friday and a special defaulter's parade on Tuesdays when the defaulters were required to parade in full uniform with shining boots and gleaming brasses. Divinity was compulsory at every level. The production of Gilbert and Sullivan's "Patience" involved twenty boys with oranges tucked inside their shirts and large sandalled feet protruding from their white robes shuffling on stage singing, "Twenty Lovesick Maidens We".

Our public school status was drummed into us continuously by Mr Elder who enjoined us to display our superiority to the rest of society. "Walk about as if you own the place," he advised us after morning prayers. The age of the school was constantly invoked although the architecture did not match Mr Elder's vision of a traditional public school. The 1930's brick buildings, designed by Giles Scott, evoked the local golf clubhouse more than it did Tom Brown's schooldays. Moor Park, where the school moved in 1933 from central London, was on the borders of the Hertfordshire stockbroker belt, studded with large, seven-bedroomed detached houses. The school buildings harmonised with a local culture of gravel drives and suburban garages. There was not a spire or stained glass window in sight.

I sought refuge in the William books and poetry. At the end of the first term, "Winter", a poem I'd written inspired by the cold winter was published in *The Taylorian*, the school magazine:

> *A driftless grey cloud*
> *Hangs o'er the sky.*
> *The breakers crash against the cliff,*

> *A wild duck from the frozen marsh*
> *Rises to meet the gathering sky.*

There were seven more verses in similar vein, culminating in,

> *A heavily timbered stagecoach*
> *Noisily rumbles by,*
> *As men with torches held aloft*
> *Scan the falling sky.*

Stagecoaches were not common in Rayners Lane nor in Moor Park, but I had been inspired by the work of Masefield, de la Mare, Alfred Noyes and local Christmas cards. My literary effusions did not save me from being ranked 22nd out of 25 in the class order, an ignominious position for one selected from the whole of Middlesex. I was ashamed of my pathetic performance, but worse was to follow.

My first school report arrived with the Christmas morning post, a delivery aimed at delivering last-minute presents and turkeys to waiting customers who usually received the deliveries with rapture. We were in the midst of family festivities with Uncle Paul, Michael and Auntie Marjorie. I knew immediately what the long envelope contained. It was the verdict on my first term's work and I knew it would be damning as my father opened it.

"Now we'll see what someone else thinks of him," my father said ominously.

He slit open the envelope, unfolded the report and began to read, then lowered his voice as it became apparent that the verdict was not favourable. I had come top of the class in History but this had not prevented Mr Baiss's withering criticism: *He has some aptitude for this subject*, he wrote, *but this does not mean his general attitude is acceptable.* I lacked concentration, attention, and diligence. The atmosphere of Christmas festivity began to cool. My father turned the report over to the back, where there were three longer paragraphs, the first by the housemaster: *I certainly hope that his conduct and general demeanour will improve next term,* an optimism followed by Mr Dutton's disapproving paragraph ending with: *His one aim seems to be to make the class laugh.* I thought this unfair since I could recall virtually no laughter during my first term. And finally there was the Mr Elder's magisterial summing up in his small, meticulous handwriting: *I must warn him that he cannot make bricks without straw for ever.* This biblical reference was initially lost on my father who knew that I was not at the school to make bricks, but its general import was clear enough. *It is my duty to warn him,* Elder stated, *that he should not squander his opportunities indefinitely.*

My father folded the report and slid it back into the envelope. He was tight-lipped. "We'll discuss this later," he said.

Uncle Paul chipped in helpfully with, "Michael's had some bad reports, but none as bad as that." Michael smirked in the background but I was glad he was with me.

I tried to pretend the catastrophe had not happened but it had and my parents were completely on the side of the teachers who were authoritative and prestigious figures. I too was on their side. They had taught me, weighed the evidence and given their verdict. I had nothing to say in my defence. I was worthless, stupid, delinquent, inattentive and lazy. I was squandering my parents' and the taxpayers' hard earned money and there was clearly something wrong with me, a near-criminal streak running through my character like streaky bacon. I felt like a condemned man standing in the dock, sentenced to be transported for seven years. I should have been sent to the Secondary Modern School at Eastcote Lane, next to the fish-and-chip shop. Instead I had been granted all the privileges that my parents never had and was throwing them away. The school verdict was virtually unanimous. There were no dissenting voices apart from the art teacher and I could tell my parents were shocked and disappointed. I had let them down and I was ashamed.

There was nobody on my side except Michael, and he was going away. Over Christmas dinner Uncle Paul announced he had been offered a job on a newspaper in Johannesburg in South Africa which he had visited during the war. He had decided to emigrate there with Marjorie and Michael. It was another devastating announcement.

"England's got nothing to offer me," he said.

I didn't feel it had much to offer me either but I was sentenced to stay.

37 Wintry Journey

My mother had always been determined to leave Rayners Lane at the first opportunity. She said she had never liked it and there was still the unresolved feud with the next-door neighbour, Mrs Bridges. Now with the end of the war, she could go.

I didn't want to move. I couldn't imagine any other place that was able to offer what Rayners Lane offered. Its boundaries seemed infinite, its texture inexhaustibly rich. A mile away there was the dump which we explored for pram-wheels and birds' nests; a mile in the other direction were the Alexandra fields where we collected frogs-spawn and newts; in the middle was the alley where we met for everything of social and collective importance. In the town were the Odeon and shops which now included a lending library, a half-shop that Brian and I joined for a subscription of sixpence a week and from which we borrowed stories by Percy F. Westerman, the Sexton Blake detective thrillers and a series of French Foreign Legion novels by P.C. Wren beginning with "Beau Geste" that we had seen at the Saturday morning pictures. What more could life offer?

But it was already changing. The two Johns had disappeared and Merchant Taylors was consuming my life from eight in the morning until eight in the evening when I traipsed home in the dark as the autumn term progressed, with two hours homework to complete every night. School had expanded from a peripheral activity to something that was taking up the whole of my life.

In search of diversion I joined the school scout troop, where the masters reappeared as scoutmasters with floppy hats and short trousers. But Messrs Cherrett, Dutton and Parsons in shorts still carried with them the rigours of classroom discipline. There was none of the anarchic, chaotic joy of Bagheera playing British Bulldog in the dusty yard at the back of the Baptist church. We tied our knots in the same spirit as we declined Latin nouns or solved quadratic equations. And I was no longer able to go to Saturday morning cinema because there was school on Saturdays, with lessons in the morning and compulsory games in the afternoon.

I accompanied my parents on trips to view prospective homes, walking along streets which were almost identical with Capthorne Avenue except I knew no one there and nothing about them. I began to assimilate the discourse surrounding the buying of houses. I learned that there are subtle differences between a house with a side-entrance and one in the middle of a row and crucial differences between a lavatory in the bathroom and one that was sitting in a room by itself. There were districts such as Wealdstone and Acton, which my mother didn't consider worthy of visiting. *Property*, I discovered was the preferred word for a house; "It's a lovely property but a little too near the main road," was the sort of imitative comment I found myself making. I unearthed an underworld of surveys and damp-courses, re-wiring and downpipes. I talked to Dad about wet rot and dry rot as we trudged up ice-covered paths to a variety of strange front doors. Underneath it all I felt very sad and tried not to think about moving. Inside the houses I followed him from room to room listening to comments on fan-shaped wall-lights and panelled doors.

When they had almost abandoned their quest for the ideal home, my parents discovered a semi-detached 1930's house in South Kenton that they liked. It had a side-entrance and at £1,800 was more than they could afford, but with extra financial effort could just about be achieved. I entered the world of financial complexity as they began the business of offers and counter-offers, percentages and fixed terms, exchanging contracts and closing dates, slipping and sliding over the ice to visit the house which had a large, pointed roof decorated with Tudor beams located on a corner with a front garden sloping to a point at the back like a wedge of cheese. Superficially it was not very different from our Rayners Lane house except that I discovered to my dismay there was no back gate and no back alley. My future disappeared in a forest of enclosed back-gardens, snow-covered and inaccessible. The lack of an alley confirmed my worst fears. My life had been in the back alley. I couldn't believe anybody would build houses which didn't have a back alley. "It's got a side-gate," my parents announced proudly but I didn't want a side-gate. A side-gate seemed to me an overrated accessory whose main purpose was to prevent me entering at the front when there was no other way of reaching the back because there was no back alley. But my parents were thrilled with the side-gate and mentioned it to everyone they met. My alley had disappeared for ever. The house was a dead end.

The winter was the most severe for fifty years and in Germany black figures of homeless refugees wandered among the ruins amid widespread starvation. The frozen ground in Berlin was blown up with explosives so that those who died on the streets could be buried. In the house the pipes froze and my father crawled about in the sub-zero attic, repairing the pipes with blowlamp and solder then wrapping felt and newspapers around them. There were frequent cuts in the electricity supply and we sat in the dining-room illuminated by candles while the slatey coal burned sullenly in the grate. We sat so close to the fire that the feeble flames mottled our shins; I developed red chilblains on my fingers that split open.

Dad became incensed at the poor quality of the coal and, ever the activist, spent one evening writing a letter to the Ministry of Fuel, wrapping up a chunk of grey slate in a brown paper parcel to accompany the letter. "Let them try and burn that," he said. My mother was not so sure about such tactics. But the coal was certainly inferior and the cold intense. A single electric bar failed to warm the kitchen. Fern-like fronds of ice appeared on the inside of the pane each morning and I blew smoke-rings in the icy air when I went to bed where the sheets had a damp, glacial quality about them and the hot-water bottle I clutched was liable to leave bulging blisters on my skin. I undressed downstairs in front of the fire, ran upstairs and curled up in a tight ball, fearful of pushing my feet down to the bottom of the bed. Getting up in the morning was an experience even more arctic. I dragged my clothes on at top speed before running down to the refrigerated kitchen where the water was frozen in the kettle and the milk on the doorstep rose out of the bottle in an elegant column of white.

In the middle of this winter we moved house which meant new rituals and a longer journey to school. I waited in the snow for a bus into Harrow, ran to the station, hurled myself sweatily into the unheated train compartment and then ran up the long drive past the playing fields which were as white and unmarked as a frozen lake. I was frequently late for prayers which meant more lines and detention on Wednesday or Saturday afternoon. Punishment became an accepted way of life and I became hardened to its pervasive presence.

The long winter dragged on. In March there was the Field Race, a major event that involved the entire school and was watched by parents. The seven-mile race, along roads, across fields and around the lake, ended with a plunge through the ice covering the River Colne. There was a pre-race meeting where we were instructed to wear underpants under our running shorts so that the watching parents would not discern the outlines of our genitalia as we emerged from the water.

I had little aptitude for long-distance running but it was not an optional event. We started in small groups rapidly thinning as we left the school gates for the wilds of the snow-covered landscape. The winter air seemed to freeze entering my lungs as we struggled across the ploughed field. It was like climbing a mountain. I spotted boys sunk by the roadside, their heads in their hands. One was leaning over a fence vomiting into the snow. We crossed another ploughed field, the muddy, freezing snow spattering up in a shower over our legs and white vests. I trudged on, feeling like a legless torso traversing fields, climbing a stile, running parallel to a hedgerow, aware of the cows staring at me with their sympathetic eyes. Dimly I was aware of parents' faces lining the route, but mine were not among them; I had concealed the Field Race from them because I did not want them associated with the school in any way. But I could sense the route was lined with overcoated fathers, fur-clad mothers and sisters with muffs, waving and cheering as we ran round the edge of the school lake down the mud-chute of the bank into the freezing water where slabs of broken ice were drifting. I waded through and scrambled out covered with weeds. I no longer cared about my frozen genitalia or anything else except reaching the end as I staggered round the edge of the white playing fields up to the finishing tape where the grass was littered with bodies, face down in the snow moaning and gasping as they were covered in blankets. I had come 110th but I had completed the course, a triumph of survival if not of athletic prowess.

Uncle Paul and Auntie Marjorie came over for their last tea before they departed on the boat for Johannesburg. There was a discussion on South Africa and the colour bar and how complicated it was with the Cape Coloured and the Afrikaners.

"The colour bar's all wrong," my father said.

"I can't do anything about that," Paul said testily. "The country's got more to offer than this one. I can't change the world."

"And he used to be such strong Labour," Mum said as we walked back from the Underground after saying goodbye. "I wonder if I'll ever see Marjorie again." She was upset. I didn't want to think that I would never see Michael again. I hated saying goodbye.

"The Daily Express" was full of stories about India preparing for independence under Lord Mountbatten, the viceroy. "He's Labour," Mum said, "even if he is royal." There were riots and killings of thousands of Muslims and Hindus.

"You see what happens when the British leave," Mum said.

"It's better if they rule themselves, even if they don't do it as well," Dad argued.

Gandhi was killed by a gunman. The paper-seller was shouting out *"Gandhi assassinated!"* as I came down the steps at Harrow on the Hill station on my way home from school.

The long winter finally turned into spring. Brian cycled to our house on his new Dayton bicycle with its derailleur gear which he had been given as a compensation for not passing the eleven-plus. So we both had new bikes. He was my last and only link with Rayners Lane.

Brian had a new fishing rod too, with a ratchet-reel.

"Come on," he said, "let's go fishing at Windsor."

We cycled to Windsor and sat on the banks of the Thames near the Eton chapel and began the first in a series of fishing trips, watching our green floats bobbing in the bright water.

We caught blue dace and grey gudgeon and red-finned roach and sometimes, if we were very lucky, gold-striped perch.

Afterwords

Len Daniel continued working as a toolmaker at Landis and Gyr in Acton, northwest London until his death in 1961 at the age of 55. His wife, Violet Daniel was left with her father who had come to live with them, until his death a few years later. She carried on dressmaking into her eighties and apart from two years in a care home, lived alone until her death at the age of 101.

Norman Daniel became managing director of Commonwealth Industrial Gases in India based in Calcutta then in Sydney Australia. He subsequently left CIG and joined Dunlop where he was purchasing manager before taking early retirement and teaching maths to police cadets at a College of Further Education in Chichester. Phyllis had three more children, Hilary, James and Susan.

Dorothy Daniel was compelled to apply for her own job as matron at Amersham hospital but was not appointed because she lacked the formal qualifications. She became a Health Visitor then retired and moved with Eileen to Corse near Gloucester where they continued their work with the Baptist church, youth clubs and tending the allotment until her death at the age of 91.

Paul and Marjorie remained in Johannesburg where Paul worked as a journalist on the *Rand Daily Mail* and *Sunday Times*.

Michael Irwin became a photojournalist based in Johannesburg working for *Time* and *Newsweek*. He also rebuilt and flew a 1942 Tiger Moth plane and as managing editor, launched City Press which became the newspaper with the largest black readership in South Africa. He married Gail, a graphic designer and they have two daughters and four grandchildren

Brian Hartel did National Service in Suez, worked for Penguin Books then changed career and became personnel officer for Firestones and subsequently personnel manager at Hoover with a major interest in industrial relations. On retirement he moved to Scotland and joined the Scottish Nationalist Party.

John Martin and John Brown, together with their families, disappeared from Rayners Lane after the war and have not been heard of since.

Victorine – Mrs Smart – moved with her husband to Wyke in Yorkshire and after hearing of Len Daniel's death while she was cooking fish on a Friday announced that although a Roman Catholic she would never eat fish again on a Friday.

Henry Goldberg went to Cambridge University where he read Natural Sciences. In his forties he took a degree in Psychology at Birkbeck College and worked in IT after a short time at Marconi's. He is married with three children and eight grandchildren.

John Daniel also went to Cambridge University where he read English and art-edited *Granta*. After a period on *The Manchester Guardian* and at the University of Minnesota he became a lecturer in English at Plymouth Polytechnic/University. By his first wife Judy he has four children and five grandchildren who are currently living in Hawaii, Minnesota, Dublin and London. Now married to writer and teacher Jane Spiro he continues to teach, paint and write poetry.